English Workbook
for
Grades Six to Eight

Ted Warren

The Teenage Edge

Copyright © 2016 by Ted Warren

Published by The Teenage-Edge & Company

www.teenage-edge.org

ISBN: 978-0-9915847-4-1

All rights reserved. No part of this publication may be reproduced, stored in a retrieval system or transmitted, in any form, or by any means, electronic, mechanical, recorded, photocopied, or otherwise, without the prior written permission of both the copyright owner and the above publisher of this book, except by a reviewer who may quote brief passages in a review.

The scanning, uploading, and distribution of this book via the Internet or via any other means without the permission of the publisher is illegal and punishable by law. Please purchase only authorized electronic editions and do not participate in or encourage electronic piracy of copyrightable materials. Your support of the author's rights is appreciated.

Printed in the United States of America

Contents

Introduction	4
Repetition of Previous Work	5
Types of Sentences and Word Positioning	8
Parts of Speech	14
Sentence Analysis	17
Phrases	18
Clauses 1	19
Clauses 2	38
Verbs	46
Nouns	60
Adjectives	65
Adverbs	76
Pronouns	84
Antecedents	104
Prepositions	107
Conjunctions	116
Punctuation	119
Fragmented Sentences and Improper Shifts	127
Irregular Verb List	146
Preparing For Tests	152

The Teenage Edge

Introduction

Grammar lessons are only valuable when you continually discover something new; otherwise, they become meaningless. It can be fun to make new examples, and discover the relationship between the words and the sentences.

It is essential that you are continually asking yourself questions. What is happening here in the language? What is the relationship we find between the words? Could the idea be expressed differently? Is this formulation typical for English, or does it break the rules?

The goal in learning grammar is to use the language well in everyday life. For example, if you are proficient in English grammar, you can read a sentence of sixty words, by Charles Dickens and enjoy it. You will marvel at his ability to combine parts of sentences into incredibly descriptive pictures. The whole text comes alive.

The following exercises are meant to set you in the right direction. They by no means provide the final answer to learning English grammar. That is up to you.

It is important that you notice that you are stretching your ability to write English. You are using better sentences, new verbs, new adverbs, new adjectives, and better nouns to engage your readers and listeners.

Ted Warren
Scranton, Pennsylvania

Repetition of Previous Work

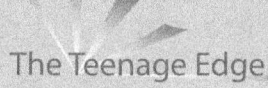

It is very important to repeat the previous year's curriculum at the beginning of the new school year. Over the summer, you have probably forgotten many details. Rather than consciously learning how your language works, you have enjoyed using it. It is normal to forget what you have previously learned.

Some people remember everything and have an unlimited ability to learn from their experiences. Others do not care what they remember, but just use the language however they like. They guess a lot and want to move on, whether or not they have the right answer. Some have cloudy memories and struggle to find the real facts. Others are very good at remembering and imagining. They like new challenges.

Notice the difference between remembering and imagining. When you remember, you try to re-experience something so that the original experience appears, in all of its details, without adding or subtracting anything. When you imagine, you do not connect to a specific past experience. You use your mind to form something new. It is your picture-creating ability. The image you create is something from your inner life that may also appear in the outer world in the future. It is the beginning of a creative process.

Every single person has their own unique ability to remember, their own ability to imagine. You are in the process of discovering your abilities and learning how to put them into action. Grammar is one of many fields where you can develop these important abilities further.

What you learned last year in English grammar may now be repeated with new examples and at a much faster pace; for example, the verb matrix on the following page is important to repeat and relearn. In this workbook, you will be asked to write sentences, paragraphs, and short stories using new areas of grammar in various verb tenses. Should you forget one of the tenses, look it up in this matrix. I have omitted *she* and *it* in the third-person singular in this matrix to save space.

The Verb Tense Matrix

	Simple	**Progressive**	**Perfect**	**Perfect Progressive**
Present	I run. You run. She, He, It runs. We run. They run.	I am running. You are running. She is running. We are running. They are running.	I have run. You have run. She has run. We have run. They have run.	I have been running.
Past	I ran. You ran. He ran. We ran. They ran.	I was running. You were running. It was running. We were running. They were running.	I had run. You had run. It had run. We had run. They had run.	I had been running.
Future	I shall run. I will run. You will run. He will run. We shall run. We will run. They will run.	I shall be running. I will be running. You will be running. He will be running. We shall be running. We will be running. They will be running.	I shall have run. I will have run. You will have run. He will have run. We shall have run. We will have run. They will have run.	I shall have been running. I will have been walking. You will have been running. He will have been walking. We shall have been running. We will have been walking. They will have been running.

Figure 1.

Notice there is a difference in the use of *will* and *shall* in the 1st person singular and plural between American English and British English. *Shall* is used rarely in everyday American English. You will find it in legal documents, business contracts, and in some prose. It is also found in suggestive statements; for example, *Shall we go?* or in music such as *We Shall Overcome*.

In British English *shall* is more commonly used.

Shall and will are two words that are used in three different ways. This makes things complicated.

1. Used to make a decision: *I shall go.*   Here you have chosen to go.
2. Used to show obligation: *I shall go.*   Here you must go.
3. Used to show the future: *I shall go.*   Here you shall go tonight or in a minute.

In England they use *shall* for the first person singular and plural. They use will for all other persons:

I shall.   We shall.
You will.   You will.
He will. She will. It will.   They will

These are more examples of using *will* or *shall* to show the future:
    I shall know more about it tomorrow.
    I shall be fourteen on Thursday.
    When shall I see you again?
    When will you be in New York?
    Shall I get you a cup of tea?
    Mary and I will go skiing today.

Shall may also be used to show a promise:
    He shall get a bicycle.
    You shall have a vacation soon.

Will may also be used to show a promise:
    I will return your favor.
    We will be right back.
    Will you help us?

Types of Sentences and Word Positioning

A. Sentence Structure

Rule 1

Simple sentences have a verb and a noun.
> She dances.

Rule 2

Simple sentences can have a verb and an unspoken noun.
> Dance!

Rule 3

Simple sentences can make sense with one or more words.
> Okay.
> We will play basketball tomorrow morning.

Rule 4

Compound sentences have two or more sentences combined by a conjunction. Remember the comma comes before the coordinating conjunctions: *and, but, for, nor, so, yet*, and *or*.
> She dances, and she sings incredibly well.

Rule 5

Complex sentences are made with a simple sentence, which is also called an independent or main clause, and one or more dependent clauses.

When the door was opened, the wind blew inside the room.

These clauses are joined either by a relative pronoun such as *who, which,* or *that* or by the coordinating conjunctions: *and, but, for, nor, so, yet,* and *or.*

The girl who is swinging on the swing is my sister.

Subordinating conjunctions may also join the clauses. A few of these are *although, when,* and *because.*

If a complex sentence begins with a dependent clause, it requires a comma after the dependent clause.

When you come in, please close the door tightly.
Although the house was empty, I went in to leave a package.

When the complex sentence begins with the independent clause, there is no comma used.

The door blew open as the wind rushed inside the room.
I know that you are doing your best to understand this.

Exercise 1

Write two simple sentences, two compound sentences, and two complex sentences.

1. _____

2. _____

3. _____

4. _____

5. _____

6. _____

Exercise 2

Write a paragraph with simple sentences. Then write a paragraph with two compound sentences. Finish the exercise by writing a paragraph that includes two complex sentences.

Exercise 3

Write two paragraphs in the past tense using at least one simple sentence, one compound sentence, and one complex sentence.

Rule 6

A compound-complex sentence may have two or more independent clauses and one or more dependent clauses.

> The dress that I wanted was in the shop window, so I bought it.
> > independent clause: The dress was in the shop window
> > dependent clause: that I wanted
> > independent clause: so I bought it.
>
> I picked the daffodils before it rained, and they stand tall in my vase.
> > independent clause: I picked the daffodils
> > independent clause: they stand tall in my vase
> > dependent clause: before it rained

Exercise 4

Write three compound-complex sentences.

1. _____

2. _____

3. _____

Exercise 5
Write two paragraphs using compound-complex sentences in each.

B. The Positions of Nouns

As the Subject: *The boy* bikes.

Direct Object: She kicked *the can*.

Indirect Object: Mike gave *the boy* a car.

Object of a Preposition: I talked with *the girl*.

Complement: Tom is *a good student*.

Exercise 6
Write five sentences, one for each type of noun placement.

1. _____

2. _____

3. _____

4. _____

5. _____

C. The Positions of Adjectives

Rule 7

When used attributively, adjectives are placed before the noun.
> She has a *brown* dog.
> The clown wears a *white* smile.

Rule 8

Sometimes adjectives appear after the noun.
> They live on an island ten miles *long*.
> My building is thirty stories *high*.

D. The Positions of Adverbs

Adverbs can be at the beginning, middle, and end of the sentence.

Adverbs of manner are placed behind the direct object or verb.
> Examples: *slowly*, *carefully*, *fast*, and *purposely*.
> He climbed over the tree *quickly*.
> He climbed *quickly*.

Adverbs of place go behind the direct object or verb.
> Examples: *below*, *under*, *after*, and *before*.
> I brought it *here*.
> She walked *there*.

Adverbs of time are usually placed at the end of the sentence.
> Examples: *now*, *tomorrow*, and *recently*.
> I saw her walk down my street *recently*.
> We will go there *tomorrow*.

Adverbs of frequency are placed directly before the main verb. They are mid-position adverbs.
> Examples:
> I *seldom* take this path.
> I *usually* walk.
> I *often* go swimming after school.
> I *always* say, "Thank You."

Adverbs, as the first word in the sentence, usually answer a question.
How? When? Where?
>   Yes, you may.
>   Still, I disagree.
>   Away with you!

Here is a long list of adverbs that can be in the front position:

afterwards, then, there, therefore, anyhow, now, so, soon, once, only, unfortunately, fortunately, luckily, evidently, personally, possibly, suddenly, consequently, usually, naturally, certainly, really, perhaps, surely, indeed, next, occasionally, accordingly, however, first, secondly, thirdly, originally, yet, and eventually.

There is also a long list of adverbial phrases that can be in the front position:

by and by, up to now, before then, until then, just then, just now, by now, every day, of course, how far, how long, how much, how often, at first, at last, at present, at least, in the future, later on, all at once, someday, sooner or later, and so forth.

Exercise 7

Write a simple story using as many adverbs in different placements as possible.

Exercise 8

Write sentences with the following adverbs in the front position:

afterwards, then, there, anyhow, now, so, once, only, unfortunately, evidently, personally, suddenly, consequently, usually, naturally, certainly, really, perhaps, surely, occasionally, however, originally, yet, and eventually.

Write a simple story in the future perfect tense using as many adverbs as possible.

English Workbook for Grades Six to Eight

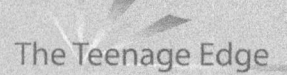

The Parts of Speech

The parts of speech are the following: articles, nouns, pronouns, verbs, adjectives, adverbs, prepositions, conjunctions, and interjections.

Articles (a)
Noun (n)
Verb (v)
Adverb (adv.)
Adjective (adj.)
Preposition (prep.)
Pronoun (pro.)
Conjunctions (conj.)
Interjections (interj.)

Exercise 9

Identify the parts of speech in each sentence, and use the abbreviations to state them.

Here are some examples:

Pro.	V.	Adj.	N.	Adv.
I	rode	my	bike	home.

Pro.	V.	Art.	N.	Prep.	Art.	Adj.	N.
She	rides	the	bike	down	the	long	hill.

1. My extremely inquisitive uncle reads three newspapers in the morning.

2. Remember to look both ways before crossing the busy street!

3. The yellow bird flew far away.

4. Emily climbs mountains in Maine and New Hampshire.

5. She rides the horse skillfully along the river.

6. After the university, Mathew and his brother, James, traveled to Europe to learn about industry and to hunt and fish.

7. William is a native Canadian, of Scotch-Irish descent.

8. "Everybody pays the same price, so they are all important," Mr. Marasco, 87, said of his barbershop clientele, which has included judges, elected officials, and private citizens.

Exercise 10

Use the abbreviations of the parts of speech to identify each word in the following sentences.

1. The mountain erupted this morning.

2. I remember we skied down the southern face of the mountain.

3. She knows the reason why he helped his brother.

4. We will leave when it starts to rain.

5. They visited the theater.

6. There is not a soldier in this army, who would not support you.

7. I am surprised you like to hike up mountains as I do.

8. It is work we want done when you are all together.

9. He bought that car because he needed more room.

Exercise 11

Compose sentences using the following types of words: noun, pronoun, verb, adverb, preposition, conjunction, interjection, adjective, and the articles.

1. one verb

_____

2. one noun, one verb, one preposition, an article, and a pronoun

_____

3. one article, one adjective, one noun, one verb, and one adverb

_____

4. one interjection, one verb, and one adverb

_____

5. one noun, one verb, one conjunction, and another verb

_____

6. one noun, one verb, one conjunction, one pronoun, another verb

_____

7. three nouns, two conjunctions, two verbs, two adverbs

_____

Sentence Analysis

To analyze a sentence, first identify the *subject*, or the *predicate*, then it is easier to find the other parts of a sentence. The predicate is the verb in the sentence. It says something about the subject.

> Subject and Predicate
> The girl *walks*.
>
> Subject, Predicate, Object
> The girls ask *me*.
>
> Subject, Predicate, Object, Direct Object
> The girls ask Mark about *me*.

A. Simple and complete subjects—simple and complete predicates

In the example below, *girl* is the simple subject, *swims* is the simple predicate.

The young girl swims enthusiastically.

The complete subject is *the young girl,* and the complete predicate is *swims enthusiastically*.

Exercise 12

Underline the simple subject or the complete subject with one line. Underline and the simple predicate or the complete predicate with two lines:

1. The green snake slithers across the rocks.

2. Mary runs into the room.

3. My old father loves to sit in his rocking chair.

English Workbook for Grades Six to Eight

Phrases

Rule 9

A phrase is a group of words that does not contain a subject-predicate combination. It is not a complete sentence because it lacks either a subject or a verb.

> The clown rolled into the circus ring. (*Into the circus ring* is the phrase). It is a prepositional phrase because it begins with a preposition. The noun *ring* is the object of the preposition.)

A noun phrase: *The Statue of Liberty* was a gift from the people of France.

A verb phrase: I *will be going* to the dance.

An adjective phrase: This is a *very exciting game.*

An adverbial phrase: They ride their bikes *without hands*.

Prepositional phrases may be used as conjunctions.

> Our helicopter is not powerful enough, *on the contrary*, it lifts off too slowly.

Prepositional phrases often act as adverbs.

> She walks quickly *through the door*.
> I will be home *on Friday*.
> I worked on the book *during the vacation*.

Prepositional phrases often act as adjectives that describe the noun.

> She received a prize *at the dinner*.
> That is the Statue *of Liberty*.

Exercise 13

Write a paragraph in the present tense, and underline at least three phrases you have used.

Clauses Part 1

There is an important difference between a phrase and a clause. As mentioned previously, a phrase is a group of words that does not contain a subject-predicate combination. It is not a complete sentence because it lacks either a subject or a verb.

The clause contains a subject-predicate combination.
Here is a phrase: with your uncle.
Here is a clause: Your uncle, *who plays for the New York Giants*, is a tough lineman.
Notice that *who plays for the New York Giants* does not make sense on its own.
If you want it to make sense on its own, you can write the following: Who plays for the New York Giants? That would be a question and therefore makes sense.

In each clause, there is a finite verb. A finite verb is a verb that has a subject: *The dog barks*. By counting the number of finite verbs, you quickly find how many clauses there are in the sentence. Once you find the clauses, you can analyze what the clause does in the sentence to discover what kind of clause it is.

A. Independent Clauses

Rule 10

An independent clause, also called a main clause, can stand alone.

> The clown ran over to the tiger's cage. (*The clown ran* is the main clause.)

Exercise 14

Make three sentences with independent clauses in them.

B. Dependent Clauses in Complex Sentences

Often the dependent clauses are easier to find than the main clause. Dependent clauses are introduced by the following relative pronouns:
that, which, whose, who/whom, and *whoever/whomever*

Rule 11

The dependent clause can have a subject and verb, but it cannot stand alone as a sentence.
>Mary Jane, who is French, moved to Pittsburgh. (The dependent clause is *who is French*.)

These are more examples:
>The newspaper, which you gave me, is one week old.
>Thank you for the support that you have given me.

Independent Clause	Dependent Clause
That is the hat	which I want.
The lady said	that she is at the station.
My sister sews	as much as she can.
The running back hits the line	as fast as he can.

Figure 2.

Rule 12

Dependent clauses do the work of adjectives, adverbs, or nouns.

An adjective clause qualifies a noun.
>That is the hat, which I want. (*Which I want* describes which hat and therefore acts as an adjective in the sentence.)
>The mountain, where we climbed last weekend, erupted this morning.

A noun clause can be a statement or act as the object of the sentence.
>The lady said that she is at the station. (*That she is at the station* tells what she said, so it functions as a noun clause.)
>I said, "Where do you live?"
>I asked her where she lives.

An adverb clause modifies the verb, an adjective, or another adverb.
> The boy ran *when he saw his friend*. (*When he saw his friend* tells time [when] so it functions as an adverbial clause. It describes the verb.)
> Walking quickly, *as only he could*, James got away. (The adverbial clause describes quickly which is an adverb describing walking.
> Tim was confident *that he would win the race*. (Confident is an adjective describing Tim. The adverb clause describes confident.)

Adverb clauses answer the questions; how, when, why, or where.

Main Clause	Dependent Clause	Type of Dependent Clause
That is the hat	which I want.	Adjective clause. (It describes the hat.)
The lady said	that she is at the station.	Noun clause. (It is the object of the verb, said.)
The boy ran	when he saw his friend.	Adverb clause. (It describes the verb, ran.)

Figure 3.

Exercise 15

Use the same subject and verb in three different sentences: one with an adverbial clause, one with a noun clause, and the final one with an adjective clause.

1. _____

2. _____

3. _____

Exercise 16

Use the following vocabulary words in sentences with dependent clauses: *nation, emergency, help, recommend, forget,* and *recurrence.*

Exercise 17

A. Draw two lines under each dependent clause and then one under the main clause.

1. She knows the reason why he helped his brother.

2. They visited the National Theater where they saw one of Ibsen's plays.

3. There is not a soldier in this army that would support you.

4. I am surprised you like to hike up mountains, as I do.

5. It is work we want done when you are all together.

6. He bought that car because he needed more room.

7. Since you are not here, I will start dinner.

8. As you are my sister, I will listen to you.

9. He worked hard, so that he could create a new product.

10. She climbed higher, so she might get a better view.

B. Write five paragraphs using one dependent clause in each. Remember that each paragraph requires at least two sentences.

Rule 13

Complex sentences have a main clause and a dependent clause. Dependent clauses do the work of adjectives, adverbs, or nouns.
> While mixing bread, my flour spilled on the floor. (*While mixing bread* is an adverbial, dependent clause.)

Exercise 18

A. Write six complex sentences with adverbial, dependent clauses.

1. _____

   _____

2. _____

   _____

3. _____

   _____

4. _____

   _____

5. _____

   _____

6. _____

   _____

B. Write a simple story about a game using complex sentences with some adverbial, dependent clauses.

Conditional clauses are dependent clauses introduced by two conjunctions *if* or *unless*.
    If Joe falls, he will get back up.
    If you are right, I am wrong.
    Unless it rains, the tomatoes will not survive.

Other dependent clauses are introduced by *as*, *than*, and *the more*.
    Success is not as easy *as you expect*.
    The waves are bigger *than I thought*.
    The more you give, the more you receive.

In addition, dependent clauses may begin with the following words: *though, although, even though, even if, whenever,* and *however.*
>   *Though he lives in Scranton*, he travels to New York regularly.
>   *Although I am fifty-years-old*, I still like to sprint.
>   *Even though you are weak*, you run very well.
>   *Even if you take my car*, I will forgive you.
>   *Whenever you arrive*, let me know.
>   *However you look at it*, I won!

The list of words that introduce dependent clauses grows larger: *because, since, in order, so that,* and *as.*
>   He bought the car *because he needed more room.*
>   *Since you work in the bank,* many people recognize you.
>   *In* order to make room on the team, we let go of three players.
>   He worked hard, *so that he could create a product.*

We also include *until, as soon as,* and *by the time.*
>   I shall wait *until you come back.*
>   We will send your money *as soon as it comes in.*
>   *By the* time I arrive, you will be there.

Remember what, that, and why.
>   *What you have learned* is remarkable.
>   *That she will fail fifth grade* is unlikely.
>   "*Why are you so obnoxious?*" was her remark.

Exercise 19

A. Write four complex sentences and four compound-complex sentences.

B. Write a simple story about eating dinner using complex sentences or compound-complex sentences.

Exercise 20

Take a passage from a book you are reading and identify the phrases and clauses in it.

Exercise 21

On a separate piece of paper, practice writing simple, compound, complex, and compound-complex sentences to show the different relationships among ideas. Make two examples of each type with four sentences each.

Here are some examples:
    I know how to bake bread. (simple)
    I bake healthy bread, and I am learning what to eat with it. (compound)
    Because I know how to bake bread, I improve my health. (complex)
    Because I know how to bake bread, I improve my health, and I enjoy the work. (compound-complex)

C. Relative pronouns introduce relative clauses

Relative Pronouns introduce relative clauses which are also called adjective clauses.

The relative pronouns are *who, whom, whose, which*, and *that*.
    Who is in the nominative case. *The girl, who runs, is my sister.*
    Whom is in the objective case. *The girl, with whom I am talking, is Jean.*
    Whose is in the possessive case. *The girl, whose hat blew off, is Hanne.*
    Which is used for animals or things in the nominative and objective cases. *The deer which crossed the road was huge.*
    That may be used in the nominative or objective cases.
    Nominative: *The fox that entered the forest is red.*
    Objective: *I saw the fox that entered the woods last night.*

Rule 14

Who, whom, and *whose* are used to refer to a person.
    He is the American, *whose* name is well known.
    She is one of the women, *whom* I know, I can trust.
    The sailor, *who* spoke, is my cousin.

Rule 15

Which is only used for animals or things. A clause beginning with *which* is usually enclosed in commas.

> The horse, *which* sped down the racetrack, is mine.
> The water, *which* filled the basement, ruined my clothes.

Rule 16

Who may be used with animals that have a name. Note the use of commas here as well.

> Our horse Thunder, *who* raced yesterday, is resting now.

Rule 17

If a collective noun refers to a team, a company, or church, *which* is used if the noun is considered singular.

> The Giants' team, *which* won the championship last year, is off to a good start.

Rule 18

If a collective noun refers to a team, a company, or a church, either *who* or *whom* is used if the noun is considered plural.

> The company, *who* are arriving today, will be delayed.
> The team, with *whom* I am playing, wins a lot.

Rule 19

That may be used in the nominative or objective cases. It can be singular or plural. It may follow the pronoun *same* and many indefinite pronouns.

> They live in the house *that* burned down last night.
> Walt Whitman is one of the greatest poets *that* lived in America.
> Do you have everything *that* you need for the camping trip?

That can be used as a relative pronoun after the word *same*.

> They wore the same uniforms *that* they used in New York.

That is used after most indefinite pronouns. For a list of indefinite pronouns, see page 94 in the pronoun chapter.

> He never does anything *that* is wrong.
> There is not much *that* you can do.

Rule 20

That is used for both a person and a thing.
> He worked hard for the soldiers and the army *that* he served.

Rule 21

That cannot be preceded by a preposition, though *which* and *whom* can.
> Here is the boat *about which* I called.
> *To whom* am I pointing?

Rule 22

What can be used as a relative pronoun.
> Tell me *what* you mean.
> He is a good racer and *what* is more, he often wins.

Rule 23

Whichever is used when there is a choice within certain items. *Whatever* is used with something that is more general.

1. Use *whoever* when needing a subject pronoun.
> Whoever wants to go to the movie meet us at the deli at 6 PM.

2. Use *whomever* when needing an object pronoun.
> Speak with whomever you like.

3. Use *whichever* when needing a relative pronoun.
> Whichever umbrella you leave behind, I will use.

4. Use *whatever* when needing a relative pronoun.
> I will do whatever I want.

Exercise 22

A. Find the right relative pronoun in each sentence.

1. Take _____ hat you like.

2. Do _____ you like to do.

3. Dance with _____ you like.

English Workbook for Grades Six to Eight

4. Tell me _____ you mean.
5. He is a good racer and _____ is more, he often wins.
6. He speaks with _____.
7. I never felt furs _____ compare with these.
8. They wore the same dresses _____ they used in New York.
9. Here is the wallet about _____ I called.
10. He never says anything _____ is wrong.
11. They visited the store _____ was closed.
12. Hank Aaron is one of the greatest homerun hitters _____ played.
13. Do you have everything _____ you need?
14. The boy _____ mother helped us is Tom Harper.
15. She is one of the doctors _____ I respect.
16. The snake, _____ coiled itself on the rock, was dangerous.

B. Write four paragraphs using as many relative pronouns as make sense.

Exercise 23

A. Write sentences with the relative pronouns *who*, *whom*, and *whose*.

who _____

whom _____

whose _____

whom _____

whose _____

B. Write two paragraphs using the relative pronoun *whom*.

Exercise 24

Write sentences with the relative pronoun *what*.

what _____

what _____

what _____

Exercise 25

A. Write six sentences with the relative pronouns *who, whom, whose, which, that,* and *what*.

Use at least six of the following vocabulary words in your sentences: *abruptly, lonely, friendly, courageous, consumption, sacrifice, anticipate, expulsion,* and *devastate*.

D. Adjective Clauses

Adjective clauses are also called relative clauses as they often begin with relative pronouns.

Rule 24

Often the adjective clause splits the subject and verb of the main clause.

> The girl, who drove the car, is just sixteen.
> The newspaper, which you gave me, is one-week-old.
> She gave a wink to the boy, who asked her to dance.

Rule 25

In spoken English and sometimes in written English, we drop the relative pronoun that introduces an adjective clause. Notice there is a missing pronoun in all three sentences below.

> Thank you for the support *you have given me*.
> The man, you want to speak with, is over there.
> I know something you do not know.

English Workbook for Grades Six to Eight

Exercise 26

A. Write five paragraphs using adjective causes as much as possible.

B. Write four sentences where you drop the relative pronoun that introduces the adjective clause.

C. Write three sentences with adjective clauses that split the subject and verb of the main clause.

D. Write two paragraphs using at least three sentences with adjective clauses.

Rule 26

The relative clauses act as adjectives. Relative clauses may be introduced by the relative pronouns who, whom, whose, and that or by the relative adverbs where, when, and why.

For example:
    The mountain, *where* we climbed last weekend, erupted this morning.
    I remember the winter day *when* we skied down the southern face.
    She knows the reason *why* he helped his brother.

Exercise 27

A. Write relative clauses using *where, when,* and *why.*

1. _____

2. _____

3. _____

4. _____

5. _____

B. Write a story about an ice cream store, using relative clauses beginning with *when*, *why*, and *where*.

E. Noun Clauses

We use noun clauses in the following ways:
The object of a verb
> I know *that you like to ride your bike.*
> I wonder *why you drive so slowly?*
> He yelled, *"The boat is sinking!"*
> Can you tell me *what the story is here?*

The subject of a verb
> *What you have learned* is remarkable.
> *That she will fail sixth grade* is unlikely.
> *"How cool is that?"* is her reply.

The object of a preposition
> The daughter listens intently for *whatever her mother says.*
> You can listen to *what he says.*

The complement of a verb: the complement of a verb adds more information to the verb.
> The fact is *that you are not paying attention.*
> This is not *what I am looking for.*

In apposition to a noun: an appositive restates the meaning of a noun or pronoun that occurs nearby.
> The truth *that we are losing the battle* finally sunk in.
> The idea *that you can win by abusing other people* repulses me.

With a number of predicate adjectives such as glad, sorry, certain, and so forth.
> I am glad *that you are here.*
> Are you certain *this is the right thing to do?*

Rule 27

Noun clauses are usually introduced by *that*, an interrogative pronoun, or an adverb.
> He said that he remembers me.
> Then he asked me what I wanted to do?
> He asked me where I was going.

Exercise 28

Write a story that starts in the past tense and continues in the present tense using as many noun clauses as possible. Use five of the following vocabulary words in your story: *proclaim, constitution, intentionally, frequently, persuade, assume, afflict, regret, apologize, confirm,* and *favor*.

Rule 28

Certain verbs are often followed by noun clauses.
Here are some examples:

> I wonder *what you are doing.*
>
> I remember *the February moon with a planet so large it looked like a cluster.*
>
> In 1916, Einstein prophesized *that far beyond our galaxy, gravitational waves and ripples would emerge from the cataclysmic collision of two black hole stars.*
>
> I wonder *whose idea this is?*
>
> I hope *what you are doing* works well.
>
> I know what you are trying to say.

Other verbs that build noun clauses are: I ask...   I tell... I love... I reply... I answer...

We place our knowledge of the noun clause in a meaningful context by summarizing the rules into a concept:

A noun clause functions as the object of a verb, the subject of a verb, the object of a preposition, the compliment of a verb, in apposition to a noun, or with a number of predicate adjectives. It can be a statement or a question.

Write your own concept of the noun clause.

The concept grows as you approach it repeatedly. Can you further develop your concept of a noun clause with new sentences?

Exercise 29

A. Create an independent clause or a noun clause that works in the following sentences.

1. I know *that you* _____.

2. _____ *why you drive slowly?*

3. He dreamed *that* _____.

4. _____, *"The boat is sinking!"*

5. _____ *that she liked me.*

6. I said, "_____."

7. Can you tell me *what* _____?

B. Write five sentences using noun clauses.

1. _____

2. _____

3. _____

4. _____

5. _____

C. Use noun clauses to enhance these statements.

I wonder...   I know...   I ask...   I tell...   I love...

I reply...   I answer...

Exercise 30

Complete the following sentences.

1. The fact is *that* _____

2. It seems *that* _____

3. _____ *what I am looking for.*

4. _____ *that she swims so well.*

English Workbook for Grades Six to Eight

5. The truth *that* _____ finally sunk in.

6. The idea *that* _____ repulses me.

B. Write six sentences using *that* to introduce a noun clause.

1. _____

2. _____

3. _____

4. _____

5. _____

6. _____

F. Adverb Clauses

Rule 29

Adverb clauses do the work of adverbs in the sentence.

Adverb clauses of manner
   I ski *as I have been taught.*
   When I have a car, I will drive *as I like.*
   She runs *as fast as she can.*

Adverb clauses of place
   Stop *where you are!*
   I will go *wherever you plan.*

Adverb clauses of time
   I like to concentrate *when I am working.*
   Before you leave the cabin, please clean up.
   He closed his computer *as soon as she arrived.*
   I shall wait *until you come back.*
   By the time I arrive, you will be there.

Adverb clauses of purpose
   I will go work *wherever you tell me.*
   He will meet him *where the river flows into the sea.*

Adverb clauses of cause
   He bought the car *because he needed more room.*
   Since you are not here, I will start dinner.
   Seeing that you know how to speak, it is your turn to give the message.
   My cousins live in the mountains *in order to hike.*

Adverb clauses of concession
   Even though you are weak, you run very well.
   Whenever you arrive, let me know.
   However you look at it, I won!
   Whether or not you read the book, you will figure it out.

Adverb clauses of comparison
   Success is not as easy *as you expect.*
   The waves are bigger *than I thought.*
   The more you give, the more you receive.

Adverb clauses of condition
   I will go, *if she asks me.*
   We will survive, *whether or not we get help today.*
   Give him an arm, and he will take a leg.

Adverb clauses of result
   I received your letter, *so now I can answer you.*
   She spoke so softly *that it was hard to understand each word.*

Exercise 31

A. Finish the adverb clause in each sentence.

1. I ski *as* _____.

2. When I have a car I will drive *as* _____.

3. She runs *as fast as* _____.

4. You speak *as if* _____.

5. Stop where _____.

6. I will go *wherever* _____.

7. Do you travel *where* _____?

B. Write three paragraphs using adverb clauses when possible.

Exercise 32

A. Finish the adverb clause in each sentence.

1. I will go work *wherever* _____.

2. He shall meet him *where* _____.

3. *Wher*ever _____ I will find you.

4. He bought the car *because* _____.

5. *Since* _____ I will start dinner.

6. *As* _____ I will listen to you.

7. *Seeing that* _____ it is your turn to give the message.

8. Some people dance *so that* _____.

9. My cousins live in the mountains *in order to* _____.

10. He worked hard *so that* _____.

11. She climbed higher *so she might* _____.

12. *Though* _____ he travels to New York regularly.

B. Write four sentences with adverb clauses.

1. _____

2. _____

3. _____

4. _____

G. Conditional clauses

The logic of cause and effect appears in conditional clauses. The first action affects the next action.

>For example:
>If you score more touchdowns than your opponent, you will win the game.

The cause is *scoring more touchdowns*. The effect is *winning the game*.

>If the rain stops, I will cut down some trees.
>If you are right, I am wrong.
>If I were you, I would not do it.
>Were Mary here now, we would know the answer.
>Had you told me sooner, I could have done it.

Exercise 33

Write five sentences with conditional clauses. Use six of the following vocabulary words in your sentences: ornament, unwillingly, fortunes, courteous, garment, consideration, chaotic, virtuous, noble, and osprey.

1. _____

2. _____

3. _____

4. _____

5. _____

English Workbook for Grades Six to Eight

Clauses Part 2

Restrictive and Nonrestrictive, Adjective Clauses

To restrict is to limit. If something is restricted, it is controlled. Parking is often restricted, and the speed you drive is certainly restricted. Official government secrets are restricted. Areas where there is significant danger or pollution have a restricted area sign and a fence to keep you out.

What can be restricted in a sentence? A sentence is the expression of an action, a feeling, or a thought. In a sentence, the meaning of a word can be so important that it becomes restricted. In other words, the adjective clause describing a word is so important to the sentence that we consider the clause to be restricted. For example: The boy *who delivers the morning newspapers in our village* is doing well at school. The fact that the boy delivers the morning paper is essential to our understanding of the boy. Essential information in a clause is considered restricted. It is not only needed, but it is essential. A restrictive clause is essential to the sentence because it restricts the meaning of the word it modifies. We do not use punctuation with an essential, restrictive clause.

There are clues to identify restrictive clauses. There will be no commas used, and it will often begin with *that*.
    The girl *who broke her leg this afternoon* is a very good skier.
    The dappled grey horse *that I know well* came up to greet me.

A nonrestrictive clause is additional information that is not needed to identify the word it modifies in the sentence. A nonrestrictive clause is not essential to the sentence. Therefore, we use punctuation to show that the information is not essential. Usually, we use commas, but dashes and parentheses are acceptable. For example: The boy, who likes to play basketball a lot, is doing well at school. The boy is the *only* one who likes to play basketball a lot. Should there be a lot of boys who like to play basketball, then we would use a restrictive clause. Here the commas show you that the adjective clause is not essential information in describing the boy and understanding the sentence.

There are clues to identify non-restrictive clauses. They will be enclosed by commas; some will start with the word, *which*. The following are examples of non-restrictive clauses:
> Uncle Joe, who is at home now, will go to the gym soon.
> Maria, I am told, loves to sing folk songs.
> My umbrella, *which has been torn*, will be useful tomorrow.

British English follows the same rules, and I think their concepts are more accurate than those of American English. They do not call adjective clauses restrictive or nonrestrictive, they call them defining and non-defining clauses. The clause either defines or does not define the noun.

The following are defining, adjective clauses:
> The boy who caught night crawlers was very quick with his hands.
> He gave a big tip to the cabdriver who went out of his way.
> This is the movie that Elias made.
> The idea that you gave to me works well in my story.

These are non-defining, adjective clauses:
> Dr. Jones, who wrote two novels, was born in Philadelphia.
> The huge oak tree which is in front of our house, will last forever.
> That rock star, whose music I like, was knighted by the Queen.
> Andrea, whom you met at the movie, is coming over soon.

All of these non-defining adjective clauses could be omitted and the sentences would make sense. Using the commas indicates that it is not essential to know that Dr. Jones wrote two novels, where the oak tree is located, whose music I like, or when you met Andrea.

Exercise 34

Decide whether or not the following sentences are defining or non-defining:
> All the stories, which were written in German, belong to Henry.
> All the stories that were written in German belong to Henry.
> She has a sister, who lives in Alabama.
> Her sister who lives in Alabama prefers the summers in the Poconos.
> The boy you spoke with is my cousin.
> She is the kindest woman I know.

Exercise 35

A. Write three sentences with restrictive/defining clauses.

1. _____

2. _____

3. _____

B. Write a paragraph with one or more nonrestrictive/non-defining clauses.

Punctuation Rule 1

As you just learned with restrictive and nonrestrictive clauses, commas change the meaning of the sentence.

> My brother, who plays football, went swimming.

This states that I have a brother who plays football, yet I did not need to say that he plays football. The main idea of the sentence is that he went swimming. *Who plays football* is a nonrestrictive clause.

If I omit the commas, I write the following: My brother who plays football went swimming. This means I am writing about my brother who plays football. The fact that he plays football is now important in the meaning of the sentence. The use of the adjective clause is now restrictive. I could have another brother or two who do not play football.

Do not use commas when the adjective clause is restrictive.

Punctuation Rule 2

Use commas when nonrestrictive, adjective clauses are introduced with the relative pronouns *who, whom, whose, and which.*

Exercise 36

Choose five separate subjects. Use that subject in one sentence with a restrictive clause, and use the same subject in a sentence with a nonrestrictive clause.

I chose the subject *goalie*. I write a sentence for you that restricts the subject *goalie*.

The goalie on our team who is Canadian blocked the puck with his stick.

Here the goalie is restricted in two ways: we know he is from Canada and that he is on our team.

Here is a sentence with the same subject that is not restrictive.

The goalie on our team, who drives a convertible, saved thirteen goals today.

The nonrestrictive clause, *who drives a convertible,* tells us that he likes cars. There could be other goalies on our team who like cars. It does not really matter that the car is a convertible.

Exercise 37

A. Write five sentences with nonrestrictive clauses.

1. _____

2. _____

3. _____

4. _____

5. _____

B. Write a paragraph with one or more nonrestrictive clauses.

C. Write a story about a bus driver using both nonrestrictive and restrictive clauses.

Exercise 38

Write two sentences that change their meaning if you use a restrictive or a nonrestrictive clause.
This is the restrictive clause.
1. The green apples that grow by the lane are my favorite.

This is the nonrestrictive clause.
2. Those green apples, which grow by the lane, are my favorite.

In sentence 1, I talk about the green apples that specifically grow by the lane as being my favorite.

In sentence 2, I point to some green apples saying which ones are my favorite; it doesn't matter much whether or not they grow by the lane.

1. _____
   _____.

2. _____
   _____.

Rule 30

Use *which* restrictively only with a preposition.
    The bucket in which I poured the milk had a small leak in its side.

Exercise 39

Write three sentences with restrictive clauses that begin with *which* preceded by a preposition.

Exercise 40

Write five sentences with non-restrictive clauses that begin with *who*.

Analysis of Clauses

A. Dependent clauses answer questions

Noun clauses answer the question *what*.
:
    She told me not to repeat my opinion.
    In this sentence the independent clause is *She told me*.
    The dependent clause is *not to repeat my opinion*
    Not to repeat my opinion answers the question: *what*!
    She told me not to repeat my opinion.

Adverb clauses answer the questions *where*, *how*, *why*, and *when*.

    She runs to school. *Where* does she run? She runs to school.
    She runs *as fast as she can*. *How* does she run? She runs as fast as she can.

She runs to find her cat. *Why* does she run? She runs to find her cat.
She runs after school. *When* does she run? She runs after school.

Adjective clauses answer the questions *who* and *which*.

The girl, who will play chess today, is gifted. *Who* will play?
The girl who will play is Nina.
The boy asked which bunch he should buy. Which should he buy?
The boy should buy the green bunch.

Conditional clauses answer the question *if*.

If you ask me, I will answer. I will answer *if* you ask me.

If you run, the dog will follow.

If you understand, I will be grateful.

I will go skiing, if you will cover the office this afternoon.

Exercise 42

A. Underline the dependent clauses, and then tell which question they answer.

1. He said that he remembers me.
2. He worked hard, so that he could create a product.
3. Thank you for the support you have given me.
4. The girl, who drove the car, is just sixteen.
5. Then he asked me what I wanted to do?
6. The newspaper, which you gave me, is one week old.
7. I will run, if it should be necessary.
8. She gave a wink to the boy, who asked her to dance.
9. Seeing that you know how to speak, it is your turn to give the message.
10. Were Mary here now, we would know the answer.
11. My cousins live in the mountains in order to hike.
12. He asked me where I was going.
13. He worked hard so that he could create a product.
14. I know something you do not know.
15. I wonder why you drive so slowly?

B. Now name which type of clause the questions introduce in the sentences above.

C. Write your definition of the various clauses.

English Workbook for Grades Six to Eight

D. Write a paragraph with each type of clause.

B. Clauses in complicated text.

Once you have learned the clauses, you will be able to use them to figure out the more complicated texts, written by our great authors, such as Charles Dickens.

Exercise 43

A. Read the beginning of the first chapter of Oliver Twist and notice how your knowledge of clauses and phrases helps you understand the text.

Oliver Twist
Chapter 1

    Among other public buildings in a certain town, which for many reasons it will be prudent to refrain from mentioning, and to which I will assign no fictitious name, there is one anciently common to most towns, great or small: to wit, a workhouse; and in this workhouse was born: on a day and date which I need not trouble myself to repeat, inasmuch as it can be of no possible consequence to the reader, in this stage of the business at all events: the item of morality whose name is prefixed to the head of this chapter.
    For a long time after it was ushered into this world of sorrow and trouble, by parish surgeon, it remained a matter of considerable doubt whether the child would survive to hear any name at all; in which case it is somewhat more than probable that these memoirs would never have appeared; or, if they had, that being comprised within a couple of pages, they would have possessed the inestimable merit of being the most concise, and faithful specimen of biography, extant in the literature of any age or country.
    Although I am not disposed to maintain that the being born in a workhouse, is in itself the most fortunate and enviable circumstance that can possibly befall a human being, I do mean to say that in this particular instance, it was the best thing for Oliver Twist that could by possibility have occurred. The fact is, that there was considerable difficulty in inducing Oliver to take upon himself the office of respiration, - a troublesome practice, but one which custom has rendered necessary to our easy existence; and for some time he lay gasping on a little flock mattress, rather unequally poised between this world and the next: the balance being decidedly in favor of the latter. Now, if, during this brief period, Oliver had been surrounded by careful grandmothers, anxious aunts, experienced nurses, and doctors of profound wisdom, he would most inevitably and indubitably have been killed in no time. There being nobody by, however, but a pauper old woman, who was rendered rather misty by an unwanted allowance of beer; and a parish surgeon who did such matters by contract; Oliver and Nature fought out the point between them. The result was, that, after a few struggles

Oliver breathed, sneezed, and proceeded to advertise to the inmates of the workhouse that fact of a new burden having been imposed upon the parish, by setting up as loud a cry as could reasonably have been expected from a male infant who had not been possessed of that very useful appendage, a voice, for a much longer space of time than three minutes and a quarter.

As Oliver gave this first proof of the free and proper action of his lungs, the patchwork coverlet which was carelessly flung over the iron bedstead, rustled; the pale face of a young woman was raised feebly from the pillow; and a faint voice imperfectly articulated the words,
"Let me see the child, and die."

from The Adventures of Oliver Twist by Charles Dickens, Boston, Estes & Lauriat, 1890.

B. Now underline the phrases with one line and the clauses with two lines.

C. Identify phrases and clauses in the quote below from *Great Expectations* by Charles Dickens, 1890.

"Well, but I mean a four-footed Squeaker," said Mr. Pumbleschook. "If you had been born such, would you have been here now? Not you" –

"Unless in that form," said Mr. Wopsle, nodding towards the dish.

"But I don't mean in that form, sir," returned Mr. Pumbleschook, who had an objection to being interrupted; "I mean, enjoying himself with his elders and betters, and improving himself with their conversation, and rolling in the lap of luxury. Would he have been doing that? No, he wouldn't. And what would have been your destination?" turning on me again. "You would have been disposed of for so many shillings, according to the market price of the article, and Dunstable the butcher would have come up to you as you lay in your straw, and he would have whipped you under his left arm, and with his right he would have tucked up his frock to get a penknife from out of his waistcoat pocket, and he would have shed your blood and had your life. No bringing up by hand then. Not a bit of it!"

Joe offered me more gravy, which I was afraid to take.

Verbs

A. Transitive and Intransitive Verbs

If the action of the verb is transferred from the subject to an object, we call these verbs, *transitive* verbs.
    The boxer hits the bag.
    The waiter writes the check.
    The girl opens the door.

These verbs become *intransitive* when there is no object involved.
    The boxer hits.
    The waiter writes.
    The girl opens.

Intransitive	Transitive
They sit down.	The mother put the food on the table.
The girls run well.	She runs the motor.
The teacher teaches.	The teacher teaches the eighth grade.
School closes today.	They closed the school due to snow.

Figure 4.

Exercise 44

A. Find the intransitive or transitive form of the verb.

Intransitive	Transitive
They sit down.	
The girls speak loudly.	
	The runner runs the race.
	They lit the fire.
I pray constantly.	
	They drove their car to the beach.
	You answer the question.

He writes.	
The tree falls.	
Lightning strikes.	
	She reads the newspaper.
	I answer the phone.
He forgets.	
	He burns the burgers.

Figure 5.

B. Describe the difference between transitive and intransitive verbs and give examples.

B. Verbs with Prepositions

Many verbs are closely related to prepositions.
These are some examples: to get *up*, to sit *down*, to knock *out*, to spit *up*, to look *over*, and to reach *behind*.

Exercise 45

A. Make full sentences with the following verbs: to sit *down, to knock out, to split up, to look over*, and *to reach behind*.

B. Make your own sentences with the following verbs and prepositions:
get around, get out, figure out, draw out, come by, look over, break out, call on, break down, care about, check into, close down, detract from, refer to, drop in, try for, look forward, call off, and *depend on*.

C. Special Finite Verbs

Rule 31

There are twelve special finite verbs that help other verbs form the interrogative, negative, and emphatic forms of speech. They also form tenses, mood, and voice:

be, have, can, do, shall, will, may, must, need, ought, dare, and used to

Here are some examples:
    He hasn't a lot of time.
    I didn't dare swim at the park.
    She ought to work hard.
    I hope to be able to go home.
    I can hear you.
    If you tried, could you do it?
    He would play.
    I might have asked you.
    Must I give you an answer?
    People used to think it was easy to read.

Affirmative	Negative	Interrogative
He needs help.	He does not need help.	Does he need help?
I speak Spanish.	I do not speak Spanish.	Can I speak Spanish?
She climbs.	She does not climb.	Does she climb?

Figure 6.

Exercise 46

Use each of the twelve verbs mentioned in the rule above in the affirmative, negative, and interrogative.

Exercise 47

Using the same sentence, fill in the missing categories.

Affirmative	Negative	Interrogative
You like to dive,	You do not like to dive?	Do you like to dive?
	He ought not to decide.	
I need to go.		
She may stay.		
		Shall I ask?
I do remember.		

Figure 7.

D. Mood

How the speaker is thinking is expressed by the mood of the verb that is used. The mood shows what a verb is doing and the manner in which the action is taking place.

There are five main moods:
imperative, subjunctive, indicative, conditional, and interrogative.

Rule 32

The imperative mood is expressed as a command or a request.
> Pass the salt.
> Turn to the left.
> Look ahead.
> Hit the ball and run to first base.
> Have a nice day!

Rule 33

The subjunctive mood expresses a wish.
> May he rest in peace.
> Be that as it may.
> The president suggested that the bill be passed.
> I wish that she were closer.

The subjunctive mood can be used when a clause begins with *as if* and *as though*.
> She speaks as though she were upset with me.
> She speaks as if she were surprised about the situation.

The subjunctive mood is used when an *if-then clause* represents imaginary situations.
> If she were closer, then she would be able to visit us more often.

The subjunctive mood is expressed when a *that-clause* suggests a demand, requirement, or request.

>He requested that she come home immediately.

Rule 34

The indicative mood is expressed by statements. This is the most common mood.

>She is listening to music.
>I speak Spanish.
>We shall run to the gym.
>As I was walking to school, I saw the bus stop by the bakery.
>I have already done that.

Rule 35

The conditional mood expresses the conditions that are given for a consequence following them.

>If we should remain silent, we will be failures.
>If I were you, I would accept the offer.
>If he were really interested in music, he would practice day and night.

Rule 36

The interrogative mood is expressed by questions.

>Do you remember me?
>Does this house belong to the Millers?

Exercise 48

A. Write three sentences in each of the moods: imperative, subjunctive, indicative, conditional, and interrogative.

Imperative

1. Learn your lessons!
2.
3.

Subjunctive

1. May you learn your lessons well.

2.

3.

Indicative

1. You are learning your lessons well.

2.

3.

Interrogative

1. Are you learning your lessons?

2.

3.

Conditional

1. If you learn in your lessons, algebra will be easy.

2.

3.

B. Describe the difference between all of the moods mentioned above.

C. Write five simple stories using one of the five moods in each story.

E. Infinitives

Rule 37

The infinitive is usually used after *to*. There are some exceptions.

This is how it is used:
    I want to jump in the lake.
    You ought to jump in the lake.
    He loves to jump in the lake.
    I will work if I want to.

This is when it is not used:
    Let me jump in the lake.
    I saw her jump in the lake.
    Don't make me laugh.
    I heard her play the piano.
    You better tell the truth.

We have four forms of the infinitive:

Active simple
Active perfect
Passive simple
Passive perfect

	Simple	Perfect
Active	To write	To have written
Passive	To be written	To have been written

Figure 8.

Here is an example:
- Simple active — I cry.
- Simple passive — The boat is missed
- Perfect active — I have cried
- Perfect passive — They have been made to work.

Rule 38

After the *special finites*, you do not use *to*. Here is an incomplete list of them: *can, could, do, did, may, might, shall, should, will, would, must, need,* and *dare*.

You dare not leave him.
I shall meet her.
He might speak Spanish.

Rule 39

The *infinitive* is used after the verbs *ought* and *used*.

She used to ski.
I ought to go.

F. Functions of the Infinitive

Infinitives act:

1. As a noun

To run is not an option.

2. As the complement of the verb

They live to fish here.
This work is to be done.

3. As the object of the verb

I want to find the clue.
You need to help me.
I should like to have been included.
He told me to ride my bike.

4. As adverbial functions:

That is not the way *to sail* a boat.
I am here *to become* an American citizen.
Work *to live*, not live *to work* my friend.

5. As adjectival functions that qualify a noun or pronoun:
   She gave me something *to think* about.
   I have nothing *to do*.
   Mary wept because she had no more games *to play*.
   These hats are not fit *to wear*.

Exercise 49

Write two sentences in the progressive tense using infinitives as a noun.

Write three sentences using infinitives as the compliment of the verb.

Write four sentences using infinitives as the object of the verb.

Write two sentences in the past tense using infinitives as adverbials.

Exercise 50

Write sentences using the infinitive as an adjective that qualifies a noun or a pronoun or as an adverb that qualifies the verb.
   For example:
   I want it to be helpful.
   I am afraid to help them.

afraid	_____
ready	_____
worthy	_____
easy	_____
hard	_____
certain	_____
possible	_____
lucky	_____
next	_____

first   _____

surely   _____

yet   _____

suddenly   _____

fortunate   _____

G. Participles

Participles are forms of the verbs that we use as adjectives or adverbs. We have progressive participles, past participles, and from irregular verbs we have perfect participles.
The progressive participle of regular verbs uses *ing*.
    We found the dolphins *swimming* rapidly.
    The rapidly *swimming* dolphins communicated as they crossed the bay.
    I heard her *playing* Bach.
    My *playing* brother scored a goal.

The past participle of regular verbs uses *ed*.
    The *adjusted* ski fit perfectly.
    My *dislocated* shoulder hurts.

The perfect participle of irregular verbs is always different: write, wrote, written.

Written is the perfect participle. We can use it in the passive voice.

    The story was *written* in 2012.

Look at the lists on pages 146 to 151 with columns of perfect participles. Some of the participles work as adjectives or in the passive tense, and some of them do not.

Here we use the perfect participle dealt in the passive voice and as an adjective.
    The cards are *dealt*. Passive voice.
    The *dealt* cards were fine for me. An adjective

    The arm was *broken*. Passive voice.
    His *broken* nose is still bleeding. An adjective.

Exercise 51

Use your list of irregular verbs on pages 146 to 151 to find twelve perfect participles, and use them in one sentence as an adjective and in another in the passive voice. For example:

    The candy was *hidden*. Passive voice.
    His *hidden* treasure is still buried in our yard. An adjective.

Rule 40

There are three types of compound participles. In all three types, the perfect participle refers to an action that has taken place before the action expressed by the verb in the sentence.

1. The present passive participle is formed by using the verb, *to be*, and a past participle. (being + the past participle)

  For example:
    The skis being sharpened will be sent by car.
    The novels being written will be presented in June.

2. The perfect active participle is formed by using the verb, *to have* and a past participle.   (to have + the past participle)

For example:
    Having done his homework he went outside.
    Having read the instructions he took the test.

3. The perfect passive participle is formed by using the verb *having been* and a past participle.

For example:
    Having been counted they all entered the exhibit together.
    The game having been finished this afternoon, the team took the bus home.

Exercise 52

Write sentences with present passive participles.

1. _____

2. _____

3. _____

Exercise 53

Write sentences with perfect active participles.

1. _____
2. _____
3. _____

Exercise 54

Write sentences with perfect passive participles.

1. _____
2. _____
3. _____
4. _____

Exercise 55

Write sentences with all three types of compound participles.

1. _____
2. _____
3. _____
4. _____
5. _____

H. The Functions of the Participles

1. Most often participles are used as adjectives.

    That is an *exciting* movie.
    He clutched her *grasping* hand.
    The fish were *rotten*.

The *torn* sails were used as tents.

2. Participles are used with the infinitive.
Remember the infinitive uses *to* or sometimes it drops the *to*.
> I like my eggs *fried*.   (to is dropped.)
> I could hear the kids *jumping* in the lake.
> She saw him *running* to catch the bus.
> We were glad to find her *sleeping*.
> It was fun to watch the sun *rising* quickly.

3. Participles are used as adjective clause equivalents
> There were a lot of kids *jumping in the lake*.
> This implies (who were jumping in the lake).
>
> The man, *riding on the bus,* forgot to get off.
> This implies (who was riding on the bus).

4. Participles can be used as adverb clause equivalents.
> *Being naturally friendly*, she easily made new friends.
> (The participle is used instead of *as she is naturally*.)
>
> *Going into the exam,* he was very confident.
> (The participle is used instead of *as he went into the exam*.)
>
> *Seeing the danger involved,* he decided not to jump in the waterfall.
> (The participle is used rather than *because he saw the danger*.)

Notice you start your sentences with the progressive participle.

Here are some other examples:
> *Walking to work*, I saw the deer in the woods.
> *Tired and dirty*, the boy scouts hurried home.
> *Loved and respected,* the children often visited their grandparents.

Exercise 56

Finish the following sentences:

1. Walking home, I _____

2. Looking for a book, she_____

3. Running to school, he _____

4. Losing my patience,_____

5. Reading the old newspaper, _____

6. Wondering where she was, _____

Exercise 57

Write two sentences in the past progressive tense using participles as adjectives.

Write three sentences using participles with the infinitive.

Write four sentences in the future tense using participles as adjective clause equivalents.

Write two sentences in the past perfect tense using participles as adverb clause equivalents.

Exercise 58

Fill in the blanks with participles.

1. We found the dolphins _____ rapidly.
2. I heard her _____ Bach.
3. That is a _____ suit.
4. He clutched her _____ hand.
5. The fish were _____.
6. The _____ conductor drove too fast.
7. The _____ sails were used as tents.
8. _____ to work, I saw the deer in the woods.
9. I have _____ too much money at the park.
10. _____ naturally friendly, she easily made new friends.
11. _____ into the exam, he was very confident.

English Workbook for Grades Six to Eight

Nouns

A. Grammatical Functions

Nouns act as the following:
- the subject of a sentence: *Michael Anna* slides down the hill.
- the direct object of a verb: I saw the *boy*.
- the complement of a verb: He is a patriotic *guy*.
- an indirect object: She told the *boy* a story.
- the object of a preposition: I spoke to the *father*.

B. Gerunds

A gerund acts like a noun, as in the sentence, *Swimming is fun*. In this sentence *swimming* is the gerund that acts like a noun. *Swimming* is a single gerund.

If the gerund is used as a phrase, the phrase may include both a subject and an object. The subject is usually in the possessive case.
Mike's learning to read was encouraging to everyone.
Their inviting him to their barbeque was cool.
Their missing the point created a crisis.

Exercise 59

Finish the following sentences that start with single gerunds:

1. Running _____

2. Singing _____

3. Hoping _____

4. Asking _____

5. Remembering _____

6. Giving _____

7. Demanding _____

Finish the following sentences that start with gerund phrases:

1. Running to school is _____

2. Singing in the choir makes _____

3. Hoping for peace is _____

4. Asking for forgiveness must be _____

5. Remembering your commitments is _____

6. Giving your best demands _____

7. Understanding the question is _____

8. Demanding help seems _____

9. Watching the movie at six o`clock is _____

10. Fishing for Canadian pike _____

11. Performing the play will give Agnes _____

12. Knowing whom to ask for _____

Exercise 60

Make up six of your own sentences with gerunds.

1. _____

2. _____

3. _____

4. _____

5. _____

Exercise 61

Make up six of your own sentences with gerund phrases.

1. _____

2. _____

3. _____

4. _____

5. _____

6. _____

C. Possessive Case

Rule 41

A few plural nouns not ending in *s,* add *'s*.
>	The men's room
>	The children's choir
>	The women's team

Rule 42

If there are a number of nouns showing possession, add *'s* to the final one's ending.
>	My brother and sister's friends
>	Your father and mother's friends

Rule 43

The possessive form is used primarily with the names of people and for some animals, otherwise we use *of*.
>	A spider's web
>	The cat's tail
>	The House of Tudor

Exercise 62

A. Make seven sentences using each rule of the possessive form.

1. _____.

2. _____.

3. _____.

4. _____

5. _____.

6. _____.

7. _____.

B. Write a story using possessive nouns.

D. Appositives

Appositives are nouns, noun phrases, or adjective clauses that rename or describe another noun used in the sentence. We use commas, brackets (also called parentheses), or dashes to emphasize the appositive.

>Forty-four Downing Street, *my address,* is well known in Wilkes-Barre.
>Jean, *my sister*, just did a backflip.
>The book (*The Last Train*) is easy to read.
>The friendly dog, *namely a German shepherd*, crossed the road toward me.

>Thomas Jefferson, *who wrote a significant part of the Declaration of Independence,* owned Monticello in Virginia.
>Thomas Jefferson (*who wrote a significant part of the Declaration of Independence*) owned Monticello in Virginia.
>Thomas Jefferson—*who wrote a significant part of the Declaration of Independence*—owned Montebello in Virginia.

Here is a list of some of the most popular appositives:
in other words, *by the way*, *that is*, *namely*, *my best friend*, *my teacher*, *my mother*, and *my father*

For instance:
>I am arriving tomorrow; in other words, get ready now.

I know Charlotte; by the way, she is an old friend.
The market starts at 10, that is, 10:15.
She has a great friend, namely, Susanne.

Exercise 63

A. Write three sentences with a single noun as the appositive.

B. Write three sentences with a noun phrase as the appositive.

C. Write three sentences with an adjective clause as the appositive.

D. Write three sentences using brackets (also called parentheses) around the appositive.

Exercise 64

Write sentences using each of the following words as appositives.

in other words
by the way
that is
namely
my best friend
my teacher
my mother
my father

Adjectives

A. Adjectives Used Attributively

Adjectives add further understanding to the noun. When adjectives act attributively, they provide the feeling or the quality of the noun. They are usually found before the noun they modify.

> She is a *trustworthy* friend.
> He is a *loving* father.
> The *long, red* feathers glisten in the sunshine.

Most adjectives can be used attributively.

Here are some examples: honest, hard-working, new, powerful, irritable, meticulous, gregarious, childlike, Canadian, famous, atomic, talented, innocent, glad, and genuine,

Exercise 65

Find attributive adjectives for the following nouns: mother, sunset, sunrise, trees, and wind. Write sentences with each.

Make seven sentences using adjectives attributively.

1. _____.
2. _____.
3. _____.
4. _____.
5. _____.
6. _____.
7. _____.

B. Adjectives Used Predicatively

Adjectives can also form the predicate with linking verbs like the verb *to be.* They follow the verb and refer back to the subject.

Predicatively	The car is new.
Attributively	She has a new car.
Predicatively	The boy is tired.
Attributively	The tired boy lay down to sleep.
Predicatively	The bird is huge.
Attributively	The huge bird grasped the fish in its claws.
Predicatively	The moon is waning.
Attributively	The waning moon is in the south.

Especially adjectives that begin with *a* can only be used predicatively: alone, ashamed, afloat, awake, aware, afraid, and alive.

Exercise 66

Write sentences using the following adjectives predicatively: asleep, afraid, awake, alone, aware, and ashamed.

1. _____.

2. _____.

3. _____.

4. _____.

5. _____.

C. Adjectives as Nouns

In the English language, many words may be used as different parts of speech. The adjective *brave* can be used as the noun *brave*.

> The brave man sits on the ground.
> The brave win our wars.
>
> The rich texture is extra soft.
> Robin Hood takes from the rich and gives to the poor.

Exercise 67

Make two sentences with each word, one using the word as a noun and one as an adjective: *wounded*, *blind*, *good*, and *educated*.

1. _____.

2. _____.

3. _____.

4. _____.

5. _____.

6. _____.

7. _____.

8. _____.

D. Nouns as Adjectives

Notice how words that normally appear as nouns can become adjectives:
apple pie, *silver* medal, *stone* wall, and *gas* pedal.

Exercise 68

Find seven more examples of nouns that appear as adjectives.

1. _____.
2. _____.
3. _____.
4. _____.
5. _____.
6. _____.
7. _____.

Rule 44

Suffixes are also used to create other forms of adjectives.

-y	storm	stormy
-ly	friend	friendly
-ful	harm	harmful
-less	care	careless
-en	wood	wooden
-ous	danger	dangerous
-able	honor	honorable
-some	burden	burdensome
-ic	atom	atomic

-ed	gift	gifted
-like	child	childlike
-al	brute	brutal
-an	America	American
-ical	Bible	biblical
-ish	Turk	Turkish

Exercise 69

A. Write sentences with the following adjectives:

honorable

burdensome

atomic

gifted

childlike

American

Pennsylvanian

Turkish

B. Find new nouns that can act as adjectives using the following endings.

-ous _____

-able _____

English Workbook for Grades Six to Eight

-some _____

-ic _____

-ed _____

-like _____

C. What is your definition of a suffix?

E. Participles as Adjectives

Many present and past participles can be used as adjectives. They may be modified by adverbs such as *very, too*, or *quite.* They can make a mood of comparison by adding *more* or *most*. Look at your list of irregular verbs for participles on pages 146 to 151. Many of them may be used as adjectives.

Progressive tense participle: You are *amusing*.
Adjective participle: She is quite *amusing*.

Exercise 70

Write a sentence using the present progressive participle as an adjective.
For example:

creeping
Progressive tense The snake is creeping.
Adjective   The creeping wolf approached the buffalo.

beginning
Progressive tense The student is beginning.
Adjective   _____

curving
Progressive tense The road is curving down the hill.
Adjective   _____.

binding
Progressive tense The ribbon is binding.
Adjective   _____.

broadcasting
Progressive tense The station is broadcasting.
Adjective _____.

burning
Progressive tense The fire is burning.
Adjective _____.

freezing
Progressive tense The water is freezing.
Adjective _____.

sinking
Progressive tense The ship is sinking.
Adjective _____.

Exercise 71

Write a sentence using the following past participles as an adjective: *lost*, *paid*, *split*, *knitted*, and *relieved*.

Here is an example using *tired*: My very *tired* child is asleep in her bed.

1. _____.

2. _____.

3. _____.

4. _____.

5. _____.

F. Forming the negative with adjectives

The following prefixes are used with adjectives to form the negative mood.

- un- unfortunate, unhappy
- in- inaccurate, incapable
- im- impossible, immature
- ir- irregular, irresistible, irrelevant

English Workbook for Grades Six to Eight

il-   illegal, illegitimate
dis-   disagreeable, disrespectful

What is your definition of a prefix?

Exercise 72

Find new examples to form the negative by adding these prefixes to adjectives.

il-   _____

ir-   _____

im-   _____

dis-   _____

-less _____

il-   _____

ir-   _____

im-   _____

dis-   _____

-less _____

G. Possessive Adjectives

	Singular Personal Pronouns	**Singular** Possessive Adjectives	**Plural** Personal Pronouns	**Plural** Possessive Adjectives
First Person	I	**my**	we	**our**
Second person	you	**your**	you	**your**
Third Person	he she it	**his her its**	they	**their**

Figure 9.

For example:
The child eats its sandwich.
We have fallen into our pool.
The boys flee their snowballs.
I fly my kite.
She freezes her fingers.
I like his car.
Where is your wallet?

Notice that you never use an apostrophe with a possessive adjective!
Write a paragraph that includes five singular forms and three plural forms of the possessive adjectives.

Exercise 73

A. Make sentences with possessive adjectives using the following verbs: *go, grow, know, lay* (to place), *leave, lead, lie, pay, raise,* and *ride*.

B. Make sentences with the following adjectives and prepositions:
crazy about, accustomed to, jealous of, afraid of, threatened by, responsible for, angry with, fond of, concerned about, taken by, designed for, made in, anxious about, married to, equal to, dependent on, encouraged by, and *offended by*.

Rule 45

Commas are not used with adjectives that are part of the noun.

For instance:
>Zora enjoyed her root beer float after school.
>(You cannot change the order of *root beer float* or put *and* between the adjectives because to do so would change the conventional meaning.)

More examples:
>We love hot fudge sundaes and banana splits!
>We go to Round Table Pizza on busy, Friday nights.
>I love to sleep under my Scandinavian down quilt on winter days.
>I have tickets to a Boston Red Sox game.
>We watch Saturday night movies.

H. Interrogative Adjectives

Whose	Whose car is this?
What	What places did you visit?
Which	Which apples are ours?
Whatever	Whatever made you marry him?
Whoever	Whoever sings there?
Whichever	Whichever peach you choose will be juicy.

For more rules on commas with adjectives see *punctuation rule 6* on page 119.

Rule 46

Like all adjectives, in English interrogative adjectives can be used for masculine and feminine persons and things. They may be part of the subject or the object. They may be followed by singular or plural verbs.

>Whose card did you find?
>Which arm hurts?
>What kind of soda do you prefer?
>What bosses must he answer to?
>Whose car is lying in the ditch?
>What cities did you visit in Germany?
>Whatever you do, never forget me.

Exercise 72

A. Write sentences with interrogative adjectives, using the following vocabulary words in your sentences: *fearlessness, invulnerable, allegedly, companion, exhausted, challenge, establish,* and *anxious.*

1. _____.

2. _____.

3. _____.

4. _____.

5. _____.

6. _____.

7. _____.

8. _____.

Answer the following questions:

1. Whose hat is this?
2. What places in New York did you visit?
3. Which apples are ours?
4. Whatever made you join the basketball team?
5. Whoever will sing at the party tonight?
6. Whose store is this?
7. What animals do you have in the zoo?
8. Whoever will work on that car?

Adverbs

Rule 47

Adverbs which tell *how, when,* and *where,* not only modify verbs, other adverbs, and adjectives, but they occasionally modify a noun.

    You have the *very* thing I want.
    Answer the *above* sentences. Above modifies the noun *sentence.*
    Is that hat *really* yours?
    We are in the *eastbound* train.   Eastbound modifies the noun *train.*

The interrogative adverbs are *why* and *how*.
    How did you find us?
    Why did you ask that?

Adverbs of affirmation
Yes	*Yes,* I know him.
Certainly	I *certainly* will.
Surely	*Surely* you understand.

Adverbs of probability
Perhaps	We will *perhaps* attend the party.
Maybe	*Maybe* I can join you.

Adverbs of negation
No	*No,* I do not know him.
Not	We will *not* attend the party.
Never	I will *never* join you.

Adverbs of quantity, amount, or number
Little	You only need a *little* salt.
Twice	She called *twice.*
Once	*Once* I decide, I am active.

Relative adverbs make a relative clause.
When	I remember *when* you came to our party.
Where	This is the room *where* Lincoln slept in Gettysburg.

Adverbs and Adjectives with the same form

Adjective	Adverb
He drives a fast boat.	The boat goes fast.
Mary is a hard worker.	Mary works hard.
I live in the Lower East Side.	The river sinks lower.
You have a straight ski.	You ski straight down the hill.
The early shift is over.	We leave early.
I found a dead bird.	The wind is dead.
You have enough perfume.	She tried hard enough.
I have a long truck.	I slept long.

Figure 10.

Can you find seven more examples on your own?

Adjectives and Adverbs with Two Forms

Adjective	Adverb
You have a bright smile.	The lights shine brightly. The lights shine bright.
This is a cheap umbrella.	I bought them cheaply. I bought them cheap.
He has a high forehead.	He speaks highly of you. He flies high.
He wears short pants.	The train stopped short. The train stops shortly.
He is a sound worker.	I sleep soundly. He beat him soundly.
Her fair skin shines in the sun.	We play fair. We play fairly.
The clear horizon seems near.	Stand clear of her. Stand clearly aside.
That was a close call.	He stands closely. He stands close.
The sharp pencil writes well.	He answers sharply. He looks sharp.

Figure 11.

English Workbook for Grades Six to Eight

Rule 48

Some adverbs are formed by adding the prefix *a*.
  shore—*a*shore
  loft—*a*loft
  broad—*a*broad

Rule 49

Many adverbs are formed by adding the suffix *ly;* some are formed by adding *-ways*, *-wards*, and *-wise*.

For example:
  day—dai*ly*
  week—week*ly*
  month—month*ly*
  year—year*ly*
  body—bodi*ly*
  side—side*ways*
  back—back*wards*
  forward—for*wards*
  home—home*wards*
  like—like*wise*

Exercise 72

A. Make sentences with the following adverbs: daily, sideways, ashore, abroad, and brightly.

1. _____.

2. _____.

3. _____.

4. _____.

5. _____.

Comparison of Adverbs

Adverb	Comparative	Superlative
near	nearer	nearest
hard	harder	hardest
soon	sooner	soonest

Figure 12.

Rule 50

Most adverbs of more than one syllable form the comparative by using *more* and the superlative by using *most*.

Exercise 73

Fill in the comparative and superlative forms of the adverbs.

Adverb	Comparative	Superlative
	More	Most
bright	more brightly	most brightly
unfortunately		
fortunately		
luckily		
evidently		
personally		
suddenly		
consequently		
distinguishably		
certainly		
decidedly		
entirely		
naturally		
obviously		
precisely		
surely		

Figure 13.

Adverbs that modify adjectives
   I *certainly* am hungry.
   The *extremely* old man lost his wallet.

Adverbs that modify verbs
   I think *brilliantly*.
   They *obviously* know the answer.
   He answers the police *nervously*.
   He writes *distinguishably*.
   Paint *brightly*.
   Fortunately I make money.
   She speaks *longingly*.
   Come here *promptly*.
   Evidently I make mistakes.
   I *rarely* sew my clothes.
   He shaves *briskly*.
   I drive *carefully*.
   He dances *gracefully*.
   The tiger fights *ferociously*.
   James cooks *professionally*.

Exercise 74

Practice which adverbs sound right when you use them to complete the sentence.
Would you like to make money _____?
suddenly
consequently
nervously
ferociously
naturally
easily
intentionally
voluntarily

Exercise 75

Practice which adverbs sound right when you use them to complete the sentence?

Would you like to go to school _____?
suddenly
consequently
nervously
ferociously
naturally
easily
intentionally
voluntarily
happily
fast

Here are two lists of adverbs:
completely, swiftly, very, too dangerously, nearby, early, rarely, so long, excitedly, timely, friendly, lonely, quietly, kindly, suddenly, finally, extremely, briskly, abruptly, loudly, legibly, almost never, too abruptly, highly talented, especially well, recently, heartily, rapidly quickly, clearly, splendidly, sweetly, bravely, actively, anyhow, boldly, calmly, carefully, distinctly, easily, equally, fast, gladly, how, intentionally, late, promptly, quietly, simply, sincerely, suddenly, together, willingly, wisely, wrongly, immediately, once, presently, shortly, soon, still, tomorrow, tonight, when, yesterday, yet, frequently, never, awfully, terribly, and frightfully.

amicably, brusquely, intently, disdainfully, dismally, begrudgingly, hastily, vaguely, sullenly, wryly, determinedly, purposefully, stridently, geographically, disproportionately, succinctly, gregariously, indeterminately, and specifically.

Exercise 76

Use the two lists of adverbs to find ones that make sense in these sentences?

1. I like to sleep _____

2. Do you listen _____?

3. Have you done your homework _____?

4. The _____ red fox crossed my path.

5. My _____ forgetful brother lost his wallet.

6. I remember to sleep _____.

7. He never listens _____.

8. Have you made your dinner _____?

9. I love to dive _____.

10. We never leave _____.

11. Have you eaten your dinner _____?

Adverbs of manner are placed behind the direct object or verb.
    Examples: *slowly, carefully, fast, purposely*, and so forth.
    He climbed over the tree quickly.
    He climbed quickly.

Adverbs of place go after the direct object or verb.
    Examples: *below, under, after, before*, and so forth.
    She walked behind my seat.
    She walked there.

Adverbs of time are usually placed at the end of the sentence.
    Examples: *now, tomorrow, recently*, and so forth.
    I saw her walk down my street recently.
    We will go there tomorrow.

Adverbs of frequency are placed directly before the main verb.
    Examples: *seldom, always, usually*, and so forth.
    I often go swimming after school.
    I always say, "Thank you."

Exercise 77

Use the following adverbs in sentences.

slowly, seldom, carefully, usually, fast, now and purposely. afterwards, then, there, therefore, anyhow, now, so, soon, once, only, unfortunately fortunately, luckily, evidently, personally, possibly, suddenly, consequently, usually, naturally, certainly, really, perhaps, surely, indeed, next, occasionally, accordingly, however, first, secondly, thirdly, originally, yet, and eventually.

Exercise 78

Make sentences using the following adverbial phrases in the front position:

by and by, up to now, before then, until then, just then, just now, by now, every day, of course, how far, how long, how much, how often, at first, at last, at present, at least, in future, later on, all at once, someday, sooner or later, and so forth.

The Adverb Game
Now you can play the adverb game in the classroom. It also works well at home or at parties. One person leaves the room. While she is out, the group decides which adverb they will act out. The person who left the room, Rebecca, comes back in and can tell anyone to do anything. Each person who is told to do something, must do it with the same adverb decided upon by the group. For example, Rebecca comes in and tells Mark, "Act like a policeman directing traffic." Mark must act it out using the adverb everyone had agreed upon. If Rebecca guesses the adverb incorrectly, another person is asked to do something different. If Rebecca guesses correctly, Mark goes out and the game starts all over.

The Teenage Edge

Pronouns

A. Reflexive Pronouns

The reflexive are:

Singular   myself, yourself, himself, herself, itself, oneself
Plural   ourselves, yourselves, themselves.

As *reflexive pronouns*, the subject in the sentence is acting upon the subject. It is essential to the meaning of the sentence.

Singular
I wash myself.
You protect yourself.
He teaches himself.
She hears herself.
The computer corrects itself.
One should teach oneself.

Plural
We wash ourselves.
You protect yourselves.
They teach themselves.

B. Intensive Pronouns

The reflexive and intensive pronouns are the same, yet they are used differently.

Singular   myself, yourself, himself, herself, itself, oneself
Plural   ourselves, yourselves, themselves.

As *intensive pronouns*, they place more emphasis on the subject. They can be removed from the sentence without it losing its meaning.

    I *myself* know what is best.
    The actor *himself* spoke with us after the play.
    You *yourselves* must fight the battle.
    My dog caught the ball *itself*.
    I bought the dress for my wife *by myself*.

Exercise 79

Use the following verbs to make sentences with intensive pronouns: *to dance, to buy, to speak, to realize,* and *to praise.*

1. _____.

2. _____.

3. _____.

4. _____.

5. _____.

Exercise 80

Use the following verbs to make sentences with reflexive pronouns: *to like, to help, to dry, to scratch, to realize, to dance, to sail, to negotiate,* and *to make.*

1. _____.

2. _____.

3. _____.

4. _____.

5. _____.

6. _____.

7. _____.

8. _____.

9. _____.

B. Possessive Pronouns

This hat is *mine*.　This hat is *ours*.
This hat is *yours*.　This hat is *yours*.
This hat is *his*.　　This hat is *theirs*.
This hat is *hers*.

	Singular	Plural
First Person	mine	ours
Second Person	yours	yours
Third Person	his, hers, its	theirs

Figure 14.

It is interesting to compare possessive pronouns in figure 15 with the possessive adjectives in figure 16. Notice the difference.

Possessive Adjectives

	Singular	Plural
First Person	my	our
Second Person	your	your
Third Person	his her its	their

Figure 15.

Compare the possessive pronouns above with the possessive adjectives in the following sentences.

    This is my hat.
    This is your dress.
    This is his sweater.
    This is her blanket.
    This is its color.
    This is our car.
    This is their home.

Exercise 81

Find the meaning in these statements, and circle the appropriate pronoun. Notice how the meaning of the sentence changes with the different pronouns.

1. Helen and Marie got onto (her, their) bus and sat in the back.
2. Most of the class carried (their/his or her) chair to the assembly.
3. The deer jumped out of (their/its) thicket.
4. The Miller family travelled in (their/its) own car to the fairgrounds.
5. Both sisters knew (her/their) lace-making craft well.
6. Each brother tied (his, their) flies for fishing in the brook.
7. The puppies ran around (their/its) mother as she lay on the rug.

Exercise 82

Write the following sentences with possessive pronouns rather than possessive adjectives.

For example: This is my sister.   *My* is the possessive adjective.
               She is mine.   *Mine* is the possessive pronoun.

This is my hat. This is mine.
This is your dress.
This is his sweater.
This is our car.
This is their home.
These are your shoes.
These were your ancestors.

C. So and One

Rule 51

So is generally used with the following verbs:

say	If you say so.
think	I think so.
hope	I hope so.
believe	I believe so.
suppose	I suppose so.
expect	I expect so.
hear	I hear so.
imagine	He imagines so.
fear	She fears so.

Exercise 83

Write six more sentences using *so* as a pronoun.

1. _____.

2. _____.

3. _____.

4. _____.

5. _____.

6. _____.

One

Rule 52

As a pronoun, one is used to stand for people or the first person I. It can be the subject or object. It has a reflexive form oneself and a possessive form, one's.

Subject	One can always try again.
Object	The song gives one a good feeling.
Reflexive	I believe one should not overwork oneself.
Possessive	That is to one's advantage.
As a pronoun	Take one or the other.
As an adjective	One day I will return.

Exercise 84

Write sentences with *one* in each of the following ways: subject, object, possessive, pronoun, as an adjective, and in the reflexive form.

Exercise 85

A. Use the pronoun *one* in each of the following sentences.

1. _____ must never give up when life is tough.

2. The movie makes _____ laugh uncontrollably.

3. I believe one should take care of _____.

4. That is in _____ favor.

5. Take _____ or nothing.

6. _____ day I will learn this.

7. I live _____ day at a time.

8. Take _____ and be thankful.

B. Now make four of your own examples.

1. _____.

2. _____.

3. _____.

4. _____.

D. Demonstrative Pronouns

those, these
that, this

Demonstrative pronouns and demonstrative adjectives are the same words. The demonstrative adjectives appear before the noun.
    Do you want to play with those cats?
    Do you want to play with these cats?
    Do you want to play with that cat?
    Do you want to play with this cat?

Rule 53

When we take away the noun, they become pronouns.
    Do you want to play with those?
    Do you want to play with these?
    Do you want to play with that?
    Do you want to play with this?

Rule 54

This and *that* are singular while *those* and *these* are in the plural form.
Those and *that* are farther away from the subject. *These* and *this* are closer to the subject.

Rule 55

Such is also a demonstrative pronoun. It can also be used as a demonstrative adjective.

Such as a pronoun:
Such is life!
The program, as *such*, is successful.
His effort is *such* that he deserves an award.
I like fruit *such* as nectarines, mangos, and pineapple.

Such as an adjective:
You do not have *such* apples.
Where do you get *such* ideas?
This is *such* a lovely day.

Exercise 86

Fill in the blanks with a demonstrative pronoun.

1. _____ is what I mean.

2. Why are you asking _____?

3. Do you need to advise me on _____?

4. _____ is my apartment.

5. I prefer _____.

6. Clean _____ before you leave.

7. The course _____ is successful.

8. His work is _____ that he deserves recognition.

9. I like games _____ as poker, checkers, and chess.

10. You do not have _____ friends.

11. Where do you get _____ vegetables?

12. This is _____ a lovely view.

13. Do you want to draw with _____?

14. He prefers to ski with _____.

15. _____ is what I am looking for!

16. We can do _____ or _____!

E. Indefinite Pronouns

The following are lists of indefinite pronouns:

> something, somebody, someone
> anything, anybody, anyone
> nothing, nobody, no one
> everything, everybody, everyone

In addition, there are the following: all, one, none, both, other, another, much, less, a few, a little, enough, each, either, and neither.

Exercise 87

Find the right indefinite pronoun or write your own sentences with the pronoun provided.

1. _____ of my brothers are here.

2. _____ of those towels will be fine.

3. Is _____ here?

4. _____ is lost.

5. _____ are here.

6. Something _____.

7. Someone _____.

8. Anything _____.

9. Can _____ tell me where to park my car?

10. Nothing _____.

11. _____ asked for this book.

12. Everything _____.

13. We buy _____ of the fruit in this basket.

14. One _____.

15. _____ of your answers are correct.

16. Both _____.

17. Please look for my _____ shoe.

18. Another_____.

19. Thank you very _____.

20. Less _____.

Rule 56

Both is applied only to two persons or things. It may be used as a pronoun or an adjective.

As a pronoun:
    I have two dolls; they are *both* new.
    I like *both*.
    Both are strong.

As an adjective:
    Both hands are strong.
    Look at *both* sides of the page.

Rule 57

Some may be used as a pronoun or an adjective: some, something, somebody, and someone.

As a pronoun:
    I will give you some.
    Some of us agree that it is raining too hard to kayak.
    Something is missing.
    I have seen somebody here before.
    Can you find someone?

As an adjective:
    Some boy forgot his sneakers.
    He drove some old car.
    It happened some forty years ago.

Rule 58

Some is generally used in the affirmative, and *any* is generally used in interrogative and negative sentences.

affirmative sentences
    I am looking for some baseballs.
    There is someone in the bathroom.
    I want to ask you something.

interrogative sentences
> Have you any baseballs?
> Is there someone in the bathroom?
> Is there anything I can do for you?
> Have you lost something?
> Can I have some?

negative sentences
> I haven't any baseballs.
> There isn't anyone in the bathroom.
> I can't think of anything I need.

no, nothing, nobody, no one, and none
> No fishing is allowed on this property.
> There was nothing I wanted to see.
> Can no one give me the answer?
> There is nobody here!
> None of us caught any fish.

Rule 59

Other and *another* may be pronouns or adjectives.

As pronouns:
> She held the candle in one hand and the cup in the *other*.
> One of my friends is Ruben, and the *other* is Raul.
> I need another.

As adjectives:
> There are *other* ways of behaving.
> My *other* brother is at the game.
> Please give me *another* piece of pie.

One another, each other
> We need one another.
> We appreciate *each* other.

Exercise 88

Find the proper pronoun or adjective.

1. She held the jib in one hand and the rudder in the _____.

2. One of my friends is young and the _____ is old.

3. We walked downtown to find _____ by the station.

4. There are _____ ways of behaving.

Rule 60

Any, *both*, *no*, *something*, and *nothing* can be used as adverbs in a sentence.

    The dog is *both* useful and friendly.
    I could not arrive *any* sooner.
    He is *no* better than her.
    I will play *something* special.
    You want *nothing* from me?

Exercise 89

Find the pronoun that works as an adverb in the following sentences.

1. That is not _____ worse.

2. The soup is _____ tasty and hot.

3. I could not leave _____ sooner.

4. There is _____ better skier than her.

5. Those cookies are not _____ better.

6. The article is _____ informative and critical.

7. I could not arrive at the party _____ sooner.

English Workbook for Grades Six to Eight

Rule 61

Some pronouns are used before uncountable nouns: *a, one, some, any, no, none,* and *little.*

> I need a bunch.
> You have one team.
> The little money I have is buried in the back yard.

Rule 62

The pronoun *few* is used before plural, uncountable nouns.

> The few people I know are on vacation.
> Give me a few dollars.

Rule 63

The pronoun *many* stands for plural countable nouns while the pronoun *much* is used with uncountable nouns.

> **Many and much can be used as adjectives:**
> We haven't much money.
> He didn't make many mistakes.

> **Many and much can be used as pronouns:**
> You have plenty of gas, but I haven't much.
> You have some friends; I have many.
> In America we have many.
> We all like her very much.

Exercise 90

Find the pronoun or adjective that works in the following sentences.

1. We lost _____ money.

2. She seldom makes _____ mistakes.

3. You have plenty of charm, but I haven't _____.

4. I need a _____ bunches of flowers.

5. You have _____ mercy.

6. The _____ friends I have are in New York.

7. I can help with _____ of the problems.

8. Give them a _____ compliments.

9. You have _____ good ideas.

10. The _____ wishes I have are for others.

11. I can ask for _____ forgiveness.

12. You always look for _____ good waves.

F. Distributive Pronouns

each, each one,

every, everybody

Rule 61

Each can be a pronoun or an adjective.

Rule 62

Every can only be an adjective, yet it combines with other words to become a pronoun: everybody, everyone, or everything.

Rule 63

Each is used when the total number is two. It can also be used when the total number is more than two.

Every is used when the total number is more than two. It is never used as two.

>*Examples:*
>We have two ice cream cones; each one tastes good to me.
>We have three ice cream cones; every one is tasty.
>
>I have two friends in town; each wants to see me.
>I have three friends in town; everyone is busy tonight.

Exercise 91

Write a simple story about a family party using distributive pronouns.

Exercise 92

Use *each, each one, every, everybody, everyone,* or *everything* in the following sentences.

1. _____ knows my brother in New York.

2. _____ must do his best.

3. I teach _____ of the boys.

4. We have two drummers; _____ is very talented.

5. We asked three dancers to try out; _____ is powerful.

6. I have two job interviews; _____ requires a completed application.

7. I have three friends in town; _____ is busy tonight.

8. _____ asks about my uncle in New Haven.

9. _____ must pay the price.

10. I teach _____ of the prisoners.

11. We have two singers; _____ comes from New York.

Exercise 93

A. Use *each* or *every* as adjectives in the following sentences.

For example: Every man on deck!

1. _____ girl must solve the riddle.

2. George Washington asked _____ soldier to continue fighting for the Revolution.

3. _____ child must play and learn.

4. _____ country has their own language.

5. _____ river cleans the landscape.

6. I like _____ solution you have explained.

7. You need _____ friend to survive.

8. _____ answer counts.

9. You really believe that _____ country will agree?

10. I like the dresses that _____ model wore in the show.

English Workbook for Grades Six to Eight

H. Interrogative Pronouns

These pronouns always ask questions. They are placed before the verb. Who, whom, whose, which, and what are the most common.

    Who knocked on the door?
    Whom did you see?
    What have you done?
    Whose are these books?
    Which do you prefer, chocolate or strawberry?

The answer to an interrogative pronoun may be singular or plural.
    Who made the snowman?
    Barbara made the snowman
    or
    Barbara and Nancy made the snowman.

Interrogative pronouns introduce direct or indirect questions.
    She wondered who was going to the dance. *Indirect*
    Who is going to the dance? *Direct*

Who is only used for persons.
    Who is arriving late?

Whom is preferred when writing.
    To whom did you speak?

Who is preferred when speaking.
    Who did you speak with?

What is most often used with things.
    What are you looking for?
    What is that?

Which is used for things or persons. Which is preferred when showing a limited choice. *What* is preferred when choosing from an unlimited number.
    Which of you girls can help me?
    What would you like to do today?

Whose, what, and *which* are interrogative pronouns that also act as interrogative adjectives. Remember that interrogative adjectives describe a noun. Do not confuse them with interrogative pronouns.

What kind of chocolate do you prefer?
    Whose hat is that?

Which game will you play?

The word *ever* may be added to who, whom, what, or which in order to emphasize what you are saying.

Whatever you like is fine with me.
Whatever!
Whoever asked you to jump in the lake!
Give it to whomever you like.
Whichever road you take will bring you to Baltimore.

Exercise 94

Write sentences with interrogative pronouns.

Use the following vocabulary words in your sentences: *infancy, conviction, proceed, muscular, description, allude, revile, brandish, blacksmith,* and *ardently*.

1. _____.

2. _____.

3. _____.

4. _____.

5. _____.

6. _____.

7. _____.

Exercise 95

A. Write two examples of adding the word *ever* to *who*, *whom*, *what*, and *which* to show emphasis.

1. _____.

2. _____.

B. Use the following pronouns three times in sentences, twice as an interrogative pronoun and then once as a relative pronoun: *who*, *whom*, *which*.
    For example:
    Who are you looking for?
    Who did that?
    The driver who stopped suddenly on the ice ended up in the ditch.

who

1. _____.

2. _____.

3. _____.

whom

1. _____.

2. _____.

3. _____.

which

1. _____.

2. _____.

3. _____.

Exercise 96

The sentences below are answers to questions. You make the questions that the sentences answer. Use interrogative pronouns in your questions.

For example:
    It was Jamie that had the answer.
    Who had the answer?

1. That is Marion, the other girl is Suzanne.
_____

2. That is Mr. Novak.
_____

3. I like comedies best.
_____

4. Kevin is a basketball player.
_____

5. It is a book on snakes.
_____

6. I am learning Italian.
_____

7. Those gloves belong to me.
_____

8. Kerry and John are skiing together.
_____

Antecedents

According to the *Concise Oxford English Dictionary, Eleventh Edition*, the antecedent in grammar is defined as an earlier word, phrase, or clause to which a following pronoun refers back to.
For example:
> The boy could not remember where he parked. (He refers to boy. Boy is the antecedent of *he.*)
> These fish are big and they fight well. (They refer to the fish. The fish are the antecedent of *they*.)
> Waking up early is necessary because it helps you be there when the fish are biting. (The phrase, *waking up early*, is the antecedent of it.)
> Mom hopes that we will wash the dishes immediately after dinner. It will mean they are not left in the sink for her to wash. (The clause *that we will wash the dishes immediately after dinner* is the antecedent of it.)

Antecedents as a word:
If someone said, "She greeted her friend warmly," it is possible that we wouldn't know who was being talked about. Who is she? Are there a few people to differentiate among? So we use the antecedent *Agnes* in place of the pronoun *she*. It now becomes *Agnes greeted her friend warmly*.

Antecedents as a phrase:
If we say, "That is so much fun," we may not understand what is meant. We substitute the phrase "going to the market," instead of the pronoun *that,* and we now know what is meant. *Going to the market* is so much fun.

Antecedents as a clause:
Steve wants to make sure that he is ready for the first day of skiing. This involves sharpening his skis.
The clause is *that he is ready for the first day of skiing*, and it takes the place of the pronoun *this* in the second sentence.

Problems with antecedent use:
When a sentence stands alone, not in the context of other information, there can be confusion as to what is meant. The use of the pronoun and the antecedent must be in proper agreement or the meaning of what is said will be unclear.

For example:
>Kevin saw Mark after his operation. (In this sentence, the use of the pronoun *his* does not tell which person had the operation. If Kevin had the operation, it should be written as *Kevin saw Mark after Kevin's operation.*

Another example:
>Both Brad and Ron saw the aurora borealis, but he saw it first. (It is not clear *who* saw it first. Keep the pronouns close enough to the antecedent, so the reader knows who or what you are talking about.)

How not to do it:
>Maria and Kerry both have new puppies. Hers is a husky.

Make sure the reader knows which word the pronoun refers to.

>How not to do it:
>
>*We saw the trains at the station, but now it is out of sight.*
>
>*The elephant and the bear were in the ring at the same time, but now it is leaving.*

I can correct these unclear antecedents.
>*We saw the trains at the station, but now the train to New York is out of sight.*
>
>*The elephant and the bear were in the ring at the same time, but now the bear is leaving.*

I like to go the diner because he has good cheeseburgers. (incorrect)

I like to go the diner because it has good cheeseburgers. (correct)

Sports are my favorite programs on TV. It is so much fun to watch. (incorrect)

Sports are my favorite programs on TV. They are so much fun to watch. (correct)

Exercise 97

Write five sentences with unclear antecedents and then write them correctly.

1. _____.

2. _____.

3. _____.

4. _____.

5. _____.

Rule 64

The noun qualified by an adjective clause is called the antecedent.

This is the baseball, *which I want to throw*. (antecedent = baseball)
The javelin *that I want to throw* is not here. (antecedent = javelin)

Exercise 98

A. Write five sentences with adjective clauses and highlight the antecedent.

1. _____

2. _____

3. _____

4. _____

5. _____

B. Write two paragraphs using antecedents that are qualified by adjective clauses.

Prepositions

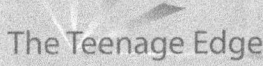

Prepositions combine with nouns and pronouns to show the relationship between them in the sentence. In a sentence, both types of words will have at least one preposition.

    I walk with you.

The preposition *with*, being used in that sentence, describes the relationship between I and you.

The reader discovers how the relationships between the nouns are determined by the preposition being used.

    I walk ahead of you.
    I walk beside you.
    I walk behind you.

There are very few rules indicating which preposition is correct to use in a given situation.

Pre means *before*. The pre-position/preposition provides the reader with the relationship between the nouns. It is the position of the nouns that is given in advance.

Exercise 99

Write 14 sentences with prepositions using one of the vocabulary words in each sentence:

pre*view*, *precede*, *precaution*, *precedent*, *predecessor*, *predict*, *precipitate*, *preeminent*, *prewar*, *prefrontal*, *premonition*, *prepay*, *preschool*, and *prelude*.

Rule 65

Prepositions may be single words or groups of words.
    I put the ball *in* my glove. (single)
    He spoke *for the sake of* many. (group)

A. Prepositions of place

Rule 66

Here is a list of prepositions and group prepositions you can compare. In the preposition game you place them between two nouns and see that some work and some do not work. Some make the sentence comical and therfore the exercise becomes a game.

up, underneath, under, towards, to, through, round, past, over, on, off, near, into, inside, in, from, down, beyond, between, beside, beneath, below, behind, before, by, at, among, along, against, across, above, and about.

And the *group prepositions* at the (back, front, side, top, bottom) of, at the beginning of, at the end of, away from, far from, in front of, in the middle of, and of.

The Preposition Game
The monkey flew ……………………… the tree.
up, underneath, under, towards, to, through, round, past, over, on, off, near, into, inside, in, from, down, beyond, between, beside, beneath, below, behind, before, by, at, among, along, against, across, above, and about.
Fill in the blank with each preposition. Enjoy your reactions!

Exercise 100

Take two of the examples above with prepositions that do not work, and explain why they do not work.

The Preposition Game Continued
The mother walks with her baby carriage ……………………… the park.
up, underneath, under, towards, to, through, round, past, over, on, off, near, into, inside, in, from, down, beyond, between, beside, beneath, below, behind, before, by, at, among, along, against, across, above, and about.

Which prepositions make sense when you use them to fill in the blank?

The boy fishes ……………………… the roaring river.
up, underneath, under, towards, to, through, round, past, over, on, off, near, into, inside, in, from, down, beyond, between, beside, beneath, below, behind, before, by, at, among, along, against, across, above, and about.

Fill in the blank with each preposition. Enjoy your reactions!

Exercise 101

A. Write your own sentences with prepositions of place.

1. ⎯⎯⎯⎯⎯⎯⎯⎯⎯⎯⎯⎯⎯⎯⎯⎯⎯⎯⎯⎯⎯⎯⎯⎯⎯⎯⎯⎯⎯⎯⎯⎯⎯⎯⎯⎯⎯⎯

2. ⎯⎯⎯⎯⎯⎯⎯⎯⎯⎯⎯⎯⎯⎯⎯⎯⎯⎯⎯⎯⎯⎯⎯⎯⎯⎯⎯⎯⎯⎯⎯⎯⎯⎯⎯⎯⎯⎯

3. ⎯⎯⎯⎯⎯⎯⎯⎯⎯⎯⎯⎯⎯⎯⎯⎯⎯⎯⎯⎯⎯⎯⎯⎯⎯⎯⎯⎯⎯⎯⎯⎯⎯⎯⎯⎯⎯⎯

4. ⎯⎯⎯⎯⎯⎯⎯⎯⎯⎯⎯⎯⎯⎯⎯⎯⎯⎯⎯⎯⎯⎯⎯⎯⎯⎯⎯⎯⎯⎯⎯⎯⎯⎯⎯⎯⎯⎯

5. ⎯⎯⎯⎯⎯⎯⎯⎯⎯⎯⎯⎯⎯⎯⎯⎯⎯⎯⎯⎯⎯⎯⎯⎯⎯⎯⎯⎯⎯⎯⎯⎯⎯⎯⎯⎯⎯⎯

6. ⎯⎯⎯⎯⎯⎯⎯⎯⎯⎯⎯⎯⎯⎯⎯⎯⎯⎯⎯⎯⎯⎯⎯⎯⎯⎯⎯⎯⎯⎯⎯⎯⎯⎯⎯⎯⎯⎯

7. ⎯⎯⎯⎯⎯⎯⎯⎯⎯⎯⎯⎯⎯⎯⎯⎯⎯⎯⎯⎯⎯⎯⎯⎯⎯⎯⎯⎯⎯⎯⎯⎯⎯⎯⎯⎯⎯⎯

8. ⎯⎯⎯⎯⎯⎯⎯⎯⎯⎯⎯⎯⎯⎯⎯⎯⎯⎯⎯⎯⎯⎯⎯⎯⎯⎯⎯⎯⎯⎯⎯⎯⎯⎯⎯⎯⎯⎯

9. ⎯⎯⎯⎯⎯⎯⎯⎯⎯⎯⎯⎯⎯⎯⎯⎯⎯⎯⎯⎯⎯⎯⎯⎯⎯⎯⎯⎯⎯⎯⎯⎯⎯⎯⎯⎯⎯⎯

10. ⎯⎯⎯⎯⎯⎯⎯⎯⎯⎯⎯⎯⎯⎯⎯⎯⎯⎯⎯⎯⎯⎯⎯⎯⎯⎯⎯⎯⎯⎯⎯⎯⎯⎯⎯⎯⎯

B. Rewrite these prepositions in alphabetical order.

up, underneath, under, towards, to, through, round, past, over, on, off, near, into, inside, in, from, down, beyond, between, beside, beneath, below, behind, before, by, at, among, along, against, across, above, and about.

Exercise 102

Write your own sentences with prepositions of place: through, round, past, on, off, near, into, inside, below, and behind.

1. ....
2. ....
3. ....
4. ....
5. ....
6. ....
7. ....
8. ....
9. ....
10. ....

B. Write a story using as many prepositions of place as possible in the paragraphs.

C. Write sentences with the following prepositions and prepositional phrases: about the story, above the wall, across the hall, against the other team, along the river, among the enemy, at the school, by the lake, inside the train, down the slopes, through the tunnel, below, beneath, beside, from, in, and inside.

A. Prepositions of Time

Rule 67

Here is a list of the prepositions of time.

about, after, at, by, before, during, for, from, in, on, since, till, until, through, throughout, to, at the beginning of, at the end of, at the time of, in the middle of, and in the midst of.

The prepositions *to, in order to*, and *so as to*, help to express purpose; they are used with an infinitive. Purpose is expressed by *for with a gerund*, e.g.
    An axe is used *for chopping* wood.
    The yacht is used *for sailing* the Great Lakes.
    The list is *for remembering* what is going on.

Prepositions make phrases, using nouns or pronouns. The phrases are usually an adverb equivalent.

I walked through the doorway.
I will go with him tomorrow.

Or as an adjective equivalent, qualifying the preceding noun.
The house with the big cabin is on the lake.
The Tower of London, among my many interests, is a long walk from here.

Notice two strong prepositions:
concerning "What do you have to say concerning him?

regarding "Regarding your article in the paper, I agree with you wholeheartedly."

Exercise 103

Write your own sentences with prepositions of time.

1. ....
2. ....
3. ....
4. ....
5. ....
6. ....
7. ....
8. ....
9. ....
10. ....
11. ....
12. ....
14. ....
13. ....

Exercise 104

Write your own sentences with the following prepositions of time: during, before, after, until, throughout, at the beginning of, at the end of, and since,

1. ....
2. ....
3. ....
4. ....
5. ....
6. ....
7. ....
8. ....

C. Prepositions and Adverbs

You can only distinguish between those words that act as adverbs and as prepositions by knowing what the words are doing in the sentence.

Preposition Joseph came *before* dinner.
Adverb   I have told you *before*.

Preposition Look *on* the table.
Adverb   I put the hat *on*.

Preposition Max is *in* the diner.
Adverb   She walked *in*.

D. Phrasal Verbs

A phrasal verb is a verb plus a preposition.
    She will *put out* the fire.
A phrasal verb can also be a verb and an adverb.
    They *made away* with the candy.
The adverbs that are attached to the verbs are called *adverbial particles*.
    For example: put down, put forward, put into, put up, put up with,
        put off, put through and put away.

Prepositions attached to verbs change the meaning of the sentence. The difference is determined by the adverbial particle, which accompanies the verb.

    I will *take up* the slack.
    Put your foot *on* the gas.
    Make room *for* your guests.
    They *put off* the game due to rain.
    Take off your baseball cap in class.
    Knock on the door.
    Put your *opinion across*.
    Make up or *break up*.
    What did you *make out* of that mess.

Notice that sometimes the noun comes between the phrasal verbs, as in the following:
Put your foot *on* the floor.

Exercise 105

Make sentences with each of the following most commonly used phrasal verbs.

You may add a noun between the verb and the adverbial particle.
For example:
She put the proposal forward.

1. *put the hands down* _____

2. *put the food back* _____

3. *put forward* _____

4. *put in* _____

5. *put into* _____

6. *make up* _____

7. *make over* _____

8. *put on* _____

9. *put around* _____

10. *put up with* _____

11. *put about* _____

12. *put around* _____

13. *make away with* _____

14. *make for* _____

Conjunctions

Conjunctions connect many parts of speech: nouns, pronouns, verbs, adjectives, adverbs, and prepositions.

A. Coordinating Conjunctions

There are seven coordinating conjunctions which connect words, phrases, and independent clauses. They are: so, *and*, *but*, *or*, *yet*, *nor*, and *for*.

A comma is needed before a conjunction when it joins independent clauses.
    Bob`s cat is smart, and its daily travel is unknown.

Remember to use conjunctions to coordinate equal ideas.
    I like to swim and surf, dive, and sunbathe in July.

Here are two sentences that are coordinated correctly:
    Marianne's apartment is simple, and her car is economy class.

    Marianne has to be careful with her illness, and she must use her time wisely.

Here the ideas are not coordinated equally:

    Marianne's apartment is simple, and she must use her time wisely.

    Marianne has to be careful with her illness, and her car is economy class.

Exercise 106

Write your own sentences using one of the following coordinating conjunctions: *so, and, but, or, yet, nor,* and *for.*

1. ....

2. ....

3. ....

4. ....

B. Subordinating Conjunctions

The most common are the following: that, when, where, while, before, until, after, since, because, if, though, although, unless, and as.
For example consider these:
    She said *that* she would paint the apartment.
    Find out *when* he will arrive.
    He danced *because* she asked him to.
    I will help you *if,* you like.
    Though he ate a lot of vegetables, he never got fat.

Subordinating conjunctions provide the relationships between ideas. We use our logic to place the ideas in phrases, dependent clauses, or words that show how they relate to the idea in the sentence:

My brother works with teenagers that need more education.
Although it was raining, we gladly walked through the park.

We place the most important information in the main clause, also called the independent clause. It is a complete sentence. The subordinate clause is not a complete sentence, but we use it to modify the main sentence.

I like the stream because there are many trout in it.
Before I leave town, I will give you a call.

Subordinate conjunctions are used with many subordinate clauses. Ask yourself, "Is the clause preceded by a main clause? Is it a nonessential clause?"

Although the restaurant was crowded, we decided to have dinner there.
Mr. Bryant, while fishing in Canada, lost his wallet and driver's license.

Exercise 107

A. Make sentences with subordinating conjunctions, using the following vocabulary words in your sentences: *autumn*, *injury*, *adventurous*, *seize*, *occupy*, *rejoice*, and *considerable*.

1. _____.

2. _____.

3. _____.

4. _____.

5. _____.

6. _____.

7. _____.

C. Correlative Conjunctions

Correlative conjunctions are used in pairs: either...or, neither...nor, not only...but also, whether...or, and both...and. We do not use commas to separate them unless a nonrestrictive clause is involved, or two complete sentences are being joined. Here are some examples:

> You must *either* join the band *or* start your own.
> You must either join the band, which I started, or start your own.
> *Neither* your question *nor* my question has been answered.
>
> It was *not only* funny, *but also* true.
> She *both* speaks *and* reads Swedish well.
> You must cross the border *or else* return to your homeland.

Exercise 108

A. Write two sentences with each of these correlative conjunctions listed above.

Punctuation

Punctuation Rules 1 and 2 are on page 4.

Punctuation Rule 3

In American English, the rule is to always put periods and commas inside the closing quotation marks.

"Her purse is hanging on the chair," he said.
"She may arrive on time," he replied, "or maybe not."

Punctuation Rule 4

The semicolon and colon are always placed outside the closing quotation marks.

"Fiddlesticks": that's what my mother used to say.
She said, "Fiddlesticks"; and I knew she had found no fresh eggs in the hen house.

Punctuation Rule 5

In American English, single quotation marks can be used inside a regular quotation. This emphasizes something!

Karen asked, "Did Sally tell you it would be 'warm' today?"

Punctuation Rule 6

The semicolon separates two independent statements that are related.

Your performance pleased me; it surprised me, and it challenged me.
She has worked hard; she will enjoy the result.
Mary slept all morning; she made it to the game on time.
I like your herbs; I would plant more peppermint.
I prefer honey; it adds to the flavor.

Punctuation Rule 7

There are rules for placing adjectives before nouns. First, you never separate one adjective from its noun:
> The warm sand fell across her toes.
> (Here we do not use a comma to separate *warm* from *sand*.)

When there is more than one adjective used before a noun, they could be coordinate adjectives that should be separatd by a comma.
> She threw her towel over her wet, scared dog.

You can reverse them, or put "and" between them without detracting from the meaning:
> She threw her towel over her scared, wet dog.
> She threw her towel over her wet and scared dog.

If there are cumulative adjectives, they may be placed according to conventional order (see below) and do not need commas to separate them.

Ordering adjectives according to conventional patterns
Cumulative adjectives are placed before the word they are describing. If more than one adjective is used, they are placed according to a particular order.
For instance, we don't say *the round big ball,* but *the big round ball.*

Here is the order for the placement of adjectives.
Number (sixteen, many, a)
Opinion (useful, stylish)
Size (huge, small)
Age (new, ancient)
Shape (round, square)
Color (blue, green)
Origin (American, Sears)
Material (plastic, cotton)
Purpose (fun, play)

Here are some examples:
> I have sixteen green plastic pens. (number, color, material)
> The school gave me two new black notebooks. (number, age, color)
> She bought a stylish American cotton dress. (opinion, origin, material)

Punctuation Rule 8

Dashes, exclamation points, and question marks go either inside or outside the closing quotation marks depending on their job in the sentence. They go inside if they are punctuating the particular quoted material. They go outside if they are not part of the quotation.

> "Is it always hot and humid here?" asked Siri. (inside)
> When he sees you, will he ask, "What is your name"? (outside)

Punctuation Rule 9

If the quoted material ends with an exclamation point or question mark, there will be no period as well.
> When she is walking slowly, he always says, "Get a move on it!"

Punctuation Rule 10

The comma is not used when a modifying clause or phrase coming after the main clause completes the meaning of that clause.
> Martin carefully knocked on the door guessing she was home. (no comma)
> Thea always does her homework on time, which helps her to keep up with the class. (comma)

Punctuation Rule 11

The hyphen (-) is used to form compound words.
> father-in-law
> warm-hearted
> eight-years-old boy

Punctuation Rule 12

The hyphen (-) is also used when a word does not fit on one line and part of the word must be placed on the next line. (frisbee, fris-bee)

> My friends from Brooklyn met us in the park where we watched the fris-bee game together in the blowing wind.

Check your dictionary for the proper division of the word into syllables.

Punctuation Rule 13

A dash (—) is used in informal English instead of a colon or semicolon to express a summary or conclusion. Beware of using them too much.

    The fans were yelling—it was exciting!

    He did not know the answer—at least pretended not to.

Punctuation Rule 14

An ellipsis indicates an omission. Three dots are used to show that we have left out words in a phrase.

    I know you meant to say . . .

    The lightning hit . . .

Punctuation Rule 15

A slash (/) separates alternative words or phrases.

    I gave it to him/her.

    We like steak and/or lobster.

Punctuation Rule 16

Parentheses ( ) are used to separate extra information from the rest of the sentence. They are also called brackets.

    Oslo (the capital of Norway) lies at the beginning of the fjord.

    Our goals are (1) to improve thinking, and (2) to spread knowledge.

Punctuation Rule 17

Using italics when typing or writing, shows emphasis.

    I read it in the *New York Times*.

    I read it in the *Boston Globe*.

Punctuation Rule 18

Quotation marks (" ") are usually double in American English. Poems, song titles, chapters, and short stories are enclosed in quotation marks.

    Have you heard "Further To Fly" by Paul Simon?

Punctuation Rule 19

When writing down a conversation, begin a new paragraph for each new speaker.
 "Do you really mean that?" I asked.
 She nodded shyly. "Of course."

Punctuation Rule 20

When quoting conversation, verbs that indicate direct speech are separated by commas from the words spoken unless a question mark or exclamation mark is used.
 "Why?" asked the little girl.
 She said, "I like the food in this restaurant."

Punctuation Rule 21

When writing conversation, the comma is put inside the quotation marks when a tab such as *he said* or *said Tom* follow the words spoken.
 "You know what you are doing," said Tom.

Punctuation Rule 22

Commas are used to separate an introductory item from the rest of the sentence. There are several situations where commas are used for this purpose:

With a participle phrase
Raising her hand, the girl stood up and gave the answer.

With an infinitive phrase
To be clear, you have much to do to clean this room.

With an appositive
The boy who can always be counted on, Alex, caught the ball and ran to the base to make the out.

After a subordinate clause
When the toaster didn't work, I knew I had a big problem.

Exercise 108

Read the text by Charles Dickens and notice the complicated punctuation.

In his working clothes, Joe was a well-knit, characteristic-looking blacksmith; in his holiday clothes, he was more like a scarecrow in good circumstances than anything else. Nothing that he wore then fitted him, or seemed to belong to him; and everything that he wore then grazed him. On the present festive occasion he emerged from his room, when the blithe bells were going, the picture of misery, in a full suit of Sunday penitentials.

Now fill in the correct punctuation.

In his working clothes Joe was a well knit characteristic looking blacksmith in his holiday clothes he was more like a scarecrow in good circumstances than anything else Nothing that he wore then fitted him or seemed to belong to him; and everything that he wore then grazed him On the present festive occasion he emerged from his room, when the blithe bells were going the picture of misery in a full suit of Sunday penitentials
—From *Great Expectations* by Charles Dickens, 1890

Exercise 109

Read the examples of the punctuation, grammar and clauses in our Constitution.

Our Founding Fathers were experts in using punctuation, conjunctions, and clauses. They spent four months in Philadelphia during the summer of 1787 debating how to establish the government of the United States of America. Along the way, they made compromises between a central government and a government that would justly represent the people within the separate states of the new country. They spent weeks finding the right clauses, the right phrases, and the right verbs.

Below are the introductory paragraphs of the first four articles. There are four areas of power they needed to balance: the Congress, the Presidency, the Supreme Court, and the States.

Notice how your knowledge of clauses helps you understand this text.

THE CONSTITUTION OF THE UNITED STATES

1787

Article I

Section 1. All legislative Powers herein granted shall be vested in a Congress of the United States, which shall consist of a Senate and a House of Representatives.

Section 2. No Person shall be a Representative who shall not have attained to the Age of twenty -five Years, and been seven years a Citizen of the United States, and who shall not, when elected, be an inhabitant of that State in which he shall be chosen.

Article II

Section 1. The executive Power shall be vested in a President of the United States of America. He shall hold his office during the Term of four Years, and, together with the Vice President, chosen for the same Term, be elected, as follows. Each state shall appoint, in such Manner as the Legislature thereof may direct, a Number of Electors, equal to the whole Number of Senators and Representatives to which the State may be entitled in the Congress: but no Senator or Representative, or Person holding an Office of Trust or Profit under the United States, shall be appointed as Elector.

Section 2. The President shall be Commander in Chief of the Army and Navy of the United States, and of the Militia of the several States, when called into the actual Service of the United States; he may require the Opinion, in writing, of the principal Officer in each of the executive Departments, upon any Subject relating to the Duties of their respective Offices, and he shall have Power to grant Reprieves and Pardons for Offences against the United States, except in case of Impeachment.

Article III

Section 1. The judicial Power of the United States shall be vested in one Supreme Court, and in such inferior Courts as the Congress may from time to time ordain and establish. The Judges, both of the supreme and inferior Courts, shall hold their Offices during good Behaviour, and shall, at stated Times, receive for their Services, a Compensation, which shall not be diminished during their Continuance in Office.

Article IV

Section 1. Full Faith and Credit shall be given in each State to the public

Acts, Records, and judicial Proceedings of every other State. And the Congress may by general Laws prescribe the Manner in which such Acts, Records and Proceedings shall be proved and the Effect thereof.

    Section 2. The Citizens of each State shall be entitled to all Privileges and Immunities of Citizens in the several States.

    A Person charged in any State with Treason, Felony, or other crime, who shall flee from Justice, and be found in another State, shall on Demand of the executive Authority of the State from which he fled, be delivered up, to be removed to the State having Jurisdiction of the Crime.

1. Read the text three times, each time more slowly than the previous.

2. Write down the independent and dependent clauses in each section.

3. Which relative pronouns are used in each section?

4. Why do you think they capitalized each noun?

5. Read each section slowly and out loud, emphasizing the content according to punctuation.

Fragmented Sentences and Improper Shifts

The goal is to be consistent in the grammar of the sentence and the paragraph. You learn to be consistent with the person, the number, the pronouns, the tenses, the mood, the voice, and the speech. If you shift incorrectly, you force your reader to question what you are saying.

A. Shifts in Person

If you shift incorrectly from the first person *I* to the second person *you* in the sentence, you make it difficult for your reader to understand.
> I am speaking with my friends when you look for the website.
> *I am speaking with my friends when I am looking for the website.*

If you shift from the second to the third person, you lose consistency.
> A student who is becoming a lawyer can understand the law when you read in the library.

This is a shift from the third person to the second person. To be consistent, you should only use the third person:
> *A student who is becoming a lawyer can learn about the law when he finds secondary literature in the library.*

Or you could be consistent with the second person:
> *If you are becoming a lawyer, you can find answers to your questions by reading secondary sources in the library.*

B. Shifts in Number

Shifts in number take place when you shift between the singular and plural in one sentence.
> The girls achieved the best results in her event.
> Correction: The girls achieved the best results in their event.

> All the winners have a prize.
> Correction: All the winners have prizes.

English Workbook for Grades Six to Eight

Exercise 110

Make the necessary correction in person and number.

1. My class promptly begins their lessons in English history, mathematics, gym, and sometimes painting.

2. Even though I dance twice a week, you will not find us on Friday afternoon at the coffee shop.

3. On Thanksgiving Day, high school football was always played; they made it a tradition.

4. The hilarious comedians in New York are usually honest but not gentle; he sometimes gets out of control.

C. Shifts in Pronouns

Notice how awkward the following sentence is.
> *A skier spends a lot of time outdoors, because they like good snow.*

What went wrong? I used a singular antecedent and a plural pronoun. That creates an inaccurate pronoun shift.
I could have written
> *A skier spends a lot of time outdoors, because he likes good snow.*
> *Skiers spend a lot of time outdoors, because they like good snow.*

Pronoun shifts may also occur when the pronouns do not match in number and person. Notice the awkward feeling you have when you read the following sentence.
> *Many boys and girls in our class like touch football; however, you may ruin your blue jeans.*

What went wrong? I used a singular antecedent (class) and a plural pronoun (you). That creates an inaccurate pronoun shift.
I should have written
> *Many boys and girls in our class like touch football; however, they may ruin their blue jeans.*

I can change the antecedent.
> *Frank likes touch football; however, he may ruin his blue jeans.*

Exercise 111

A. Write five sentences with improper pronoun shifts and correct them.

1. _____.

2. _____.

3. _____.

4. _____.

5. _____.

B. Listen to people speaking during the day and find some good examples.

D. Shifts in Tenses

Being consistent with tenses is very important for your reader. You learn to stay in the correct tense in a sentence, until you make a consistent shift.
An inconsistent shift:
The boat cruised up the river, and the shoreline changes dramatically.
Consistent:
The boat cruised up the river, and the shoreline changed dramatically.

An inconsistent shift:
The clouds flow across the sky, but they became darker and darker.
Consistent:
The clouds flow across the sky; they are becoming darker and darker.

Recognize and Correct Inappropriate Shifts in Verb Tense in Texts

You may set your reader in the past tense and then use the present tense in the following sentences and paragraphs.

Consistent: In his newspaper article, Robert Field criticizes the new water plant, and questions whether it should be so close to the school.

Inconsistent: In his newspaper article, Robert Field criticized the new water plant, and questions whether it should be so close to the school.

English Workbook for Grades Six to Eight

Exercise 112

A. Write ten sentences with inconsistent shifts in verb tenses and correct them.

1. _____.

2. _____.

3. _____.

4. _____.

5. _____.

6. _____.

7. _____.

8. _____.

9. _____.

10. _____.

B. Write a text with some inappropriate shifts in verb tense and then correct them.

E. Shifts in Mood

Rule 68

The subjunctive mood expresses a wish.
    May he rest in peace.
    Be that as it may.
    The president suggested that the bill be passed.
    I wish that she were closer.

The subjunctive mood can be been used when a clause begins with *as if* and *as though*.
> She speaks as though she were upset with me.
> She speaks as if she were surprised about the situation.

It is used when an *if-then clause* represents imaginary situations.
> If she were closer, she would be able to visit us more often.

The subjunctive mood is expressed when a *that-clause* suggests a demand, requirement, or request.
> He requested that she come home immediately.

There are three moods that show three different attitudes:
- The indicative mood is a straight-forward statement.
- The imperative mood is a command.
- The subjunctive mood is doubtful, wishful, or conditional.

In the subjunctive mood, we often use *if* and *were*.
> *It were* is used rather than *it was*. *I were* is used rather than *I was*.
> If I were young, I would go running more often.
> If it were not for you, I would never have experienced this performance.
> If they were not on our side, we probably would have made more mistakes.

F. Improper shifts in mood

1. Here is an inconsistent shift from the subjunctive to the indicative mood.
    If he were more mature, he will be a good leader.
If he were more mature is a conditional, subjunctive statement.
He will be a good leader is an indicative statement.
Do you see the inconsistency in moods when they are put together in one sentence?
To be consistent, you could write: *If he were more mature, he would be a good leader.*
Now this sentence has a consistently subjunctive mood.

2. Here is an inconsistent shift from the imperative to the indicative mood.
    Eat your spinach, you will be stronger than Popeye.

You will be stronger than Popeye is an indicative statement.
Eat your spinach is an imperative statement.

To be consistently imperative you could write: *Eat your spinach*; *you will be stronger than Popeye.*
Now this sentence has a consistently imperative mood.

3. Here is another example of shifting incorrectly from the imperative mood to the indicative mood.
     Pick me up at seven, and then you should drive me to work.
To be consistently imperative you could write: Pick me up at seven, and drive me to work.

4. Here is an inconsistent shift from the imperative to the subjunctive mood.
    Act your age, and you may be a better friend.

Act your age, is an imperative statement.
And you may be a better friend is a subjunctive statement.

To be consistent you could write: *Act your age, and be a better friend.*
Now this sentence has a consistently imperative mood.

Exercise 113

Correct the following sentences that show an improper shift in mood.

1. If I was mistaken, I would admit it.

2. If I was you, I would not take it.

3. Do your homework, and you must write the answers clearly.

4. make more examples

Exercise 114

A. To freshen your memory of all three moods and their differences write three sentences with each mood: the indicative mood, the imperative mood, and the subjunctive mood.

1. _____.

2. _____.

3. _____.

4. _____.

5. _____.

6. _____.

7. _____.

8. _____.

9. _____.

English Workbook for Grades Six to Eight

B. Now write six sentences with improper shifts and correct them.

1. _____.

2. _____.

3. _____.

4. _____.

5. _____.

6. _____.

C. Now write six sentences in the future tense with improper shifts.

1. _____.

2. _____.

3. _____.

4. _____.

5. _____.

6. _____.

F. Shifts in Voice

Transitive verbs transfer the action in the sentence from a subject to an object. These actions may be active or passive.

The cow was milked is a passive action.
The cow wags its tail is an active action.

In a single sentence, you need to be consistent with one voice or the other. Otherwise, you confuse your reader.

Inconsistent: She skied quickly down the mountain, and thought the race was won.
Consistent: She skied quickly down the mountain, and thought she had won the race.

You can be consistent by breaking one sentence into two sentences: She skied quickly down the mountain. She thought she had won the race.

Inconsistent: *The circus arrived in town, and it was rumored the clown had found a gold ring.* This sentence shifts from the active to the passive voice.
Consistent: T*he circus arrived in town, and announced that the clown had found a gold ring.*

Exercise 115

Correct the shifts in mood, voice, and tense in the following sentences:

1. Schools have always been attracted by the language of colleges; for example, and it often will have used terms such as, informational, argumentative, and narrative writing. (tense)

2. The movie is far from comical in that it showed true hunger. (tense)

3. If there were any doubt left about the winner of the Super Bowl, the replay shows that the Giants' receiver was in bounds when he caught the ball. (mood)

4. The parade arrived in town, and it was believed the floats had used powerful load-systems. (voice)

5. Children use television language, and comical voices are often imitated unknowingly. (tense)

B. Write your own examples with two sentences that do not shift in mood, voice, and tense.

Exercise 116

Which of the following sentences are consistent in mood and voice?

A. Passive Voice/Active Voice

1. Martin Luther King preached non-violence, and changes were made.
2. Martin Luther King preached non-violence, and made changes.
3. Non-violence was preached powerfully by Mahatma Gandhi, and cultural changes were made.

B. Subjunctive/Indicative

1. The father insisted that his daughter wear a raincoat and puts on a rain hat.
2. The mother insisted that her daughter wear a raincoat and put on a rain hat.

C. Conditional/Unconditional

1. If there were more jobs, people will invest more in their education.
2. If there were more jobs, people would invest more in their education.

D. Impersonal/Personal (Informal/Formal)

1. You might consider the consequences of driving fast, and you also want to be careful if someone else speeds.
2. You might consider the consequences of driving fast, and you might also consider the consequences of speeding.
3. You might want to think about what'll happen if you drive fast, and you also want to consider the consequences if you speed.

G. Recognize and Correct Inappropriate Shifts in Speech

Direct and indirect speech
The verbs must change when you move from direct speech to indirect speech or from indirect speech to direct speech. This may be confused and cause inappropriate shifts in the sentence.
> The boy asked, "Is it raining outside?" (direct speech)
> The boy asked whether it was raining outside. (indirect speech)

Exercise 117

A. Change the following quotations to indirect speech and improve the sentence.

1. My grandmother gave us warm porridge for breakfast because "I know it makes us healthier."
   _____

2. I am sure the news is true because the more I read, "The writer argues better."
   _____

3. The girl wrote a nice letter to her friend and said, "Do you realize how much I like you?"
   _____

4. He always rides his bike to school so that "my mother does not need to drive me."
   _____

5. My teacher writes clearly on the board in order to "teach him how to spell and formulate my sentences better."
   _____

B. Make three sentences with shifting voice and then write the correct speech.

1. _____.

2. _____.

3. _____.

English Workbook for Grades Six to Eight

H. Inappropriate shifts in tone

Shifts in tone come from the speaker's attitude toward the subject he addresses. It is derived from diction: which verb you use, the structure of the sentence, the mood, or voice you may use.

An incorrect example:

    In his newspaper article, Sandy Curtis writes a scathing criticism of the oil companies' pollution of our ground water, an opinion we just have to support.

Exercise 118

Correct any shifts in these sentences to make the message clearer.

1. Can you think of someone who is so funny that he made people laugh easily, not very modest, and unfriendly with others?

2. You need to think of two places you could have lost the wallet: one is in your car and the other after you entered the store.

3. Children become excited by water more easily and tend to play longer than adults.

4. Tigers have the patience of saints and run powerfully in the hunt.

5. The angry store owner asked the boy politely if he could leave.

I. Parallel Structure in Words and Phrases

Some correct examples of parallel structure of words and phrases include the following:

    Joanna likes singing, swimming, and diving.
    Susan wanted to make sure that she spoke clearly, entertainingly, and persuasively.
    Christian was a good player because he was never tired, he was very motivated, and he was able to attack when necessary.

Exercise 119

Correct the following examples of incorrect parallel structure of words and phrases. Notice that a word or a phrase is used that is very different from the other words or phrases. They do not run parallel as the examples above, but point in another direction.

1. Andrew likes to fish, hunt, and he played a lot of basketball.

___

2. Joanna likes singing, swimming, and to dive.

___

3. Susan wanted to make sure that she spoke clearly, entertainingly, and she speaks persuasively.

___

4. Christian is a good soccer player because he was never tired, he was not very motivated, and he was unable to attack when necessary.

___

5. Amanda wanted to finish her homework, take a walk, and to be in bed by ten o`clock.

___

6. Tana likes to dance, play the guitar, and she was voted class representative.

___

7. Today it is warm, sunny, and must rain soon.
___

8. Christian is an honest, caring, and surprises everyone with his jokes.
___

9. The rhinos stamped their feet, roaring and charged.
___

10. Tana works hard, runs daily, and is following her friends in the park.
___

11. Harry has a new scooter, a new soccer ball, and is riding his new bike to school to meet his buddy.
___

J. Mixed Constructions

If a sentence begins with one grammatical structure and shifts to another grammatical structure, we call it a mixed construction.

Here are some incompatible sentence parts that confuse readers.

A. "The fact that"—this is a noun phrase that acts as a subject or an object.
It is used in this way: The fact that ski boots are as important for skiing as skis. *Here the writer thought the subject was "ski boots" when it was really "the fact that." Therefore, this is not a complete sentence.*
Correct: The fact that ski boots are as important to skiing as skis is never overlooked by an experienced skier.
Correct: Ski boots are as important for skiing as skis.

B. Adverbial clauses—an adverb clause that begins with a subordinating conjunction.
When, because, or although can't serve as a subject. Here is an example: When a team is successful, victory pleases owners, players, and fans alike. *Successful* is serving as an adjective modifying *team* instead of acting as the last word of the adverbial phrase.
Correct: When a team is successful, the victory pleases owners, players, and fans alike.
Correct: A successful team pleases owners, players, and fans alike.

C. Prepositional phrases—the object of a prepositional phrase, which is a noun, cannot function as the subject of a sentence.
Example: By dreaming about your vacation can give you something to look forward to.
By dreaming about your vacation is a prepositional phrase. *Your* vacation is actually the end of the prepositional phrase. In the sentence above, *your vacation* was used as the object of the prepositional phrase and also as the subject of the sentence. This is not possible.
Correct: Dreaming about your vacation can give you something to look forward to.
(The whole phrase "dreaming about your vacation" becomes the subject of the sentence; there is no longer a prepositional phrase.)
Correct: By dreaming about your vacation, you can look forward to something.
(The prepositional phrase remains and *you* is now an appropriate pronoun that serves as the subject of the sentence.)

D. Maintain consistent relations between subjects and predicates, especially with the verb "to be."
In the sentence "The child is joyful," the verb "to be" is acting as a linking verb. It means that the subject, *the child*, is equal to its complement *joyful*.
If the subject and its complement do not match, the verb is incorrect.
For example: *The computer is keenly aware of your personal preferences.* A computer cannot be keenly aware; people can be.
Correction: Target marketing programs help companies become keenly aware of your personal preferences.
Correction: Aided by target marketing programs, companies have become keenly aware of your personal preferences.

Exercise 120

A. Correct these sentences for mixed constructions.

1. The fact that lions and bear were running through the town after the flood.

   _____

2. When the stars of the big dipper became visible and created a constellation in the northern sky.

   _____

4. With the right lures, northern pike could be caught and eaten for breakfast.

   _____

5. One sign of the Fourth of July was when the fireworks resounded from village to village and when they try to outdo each other.

   _____

6. The cookies attached to your browser are keenly aware of your personal preferences.

   _____

B. Make three mixed constructions of your own and then correct them.

K. Fragmented Sentences

If a sentence has no subject or no verb, it is incomplete or fragmented. In fragmented sentences, the relationship between clauses and phrases is not correct. Fragments are not logical.

Some sentences run on!
   I grill eat and go to the movies.

Do we know what you are really trying to say? Use punctuation to improve your logic.
   I grill, eat, and go to the movies.

Or make two sentences.
   Tonight I will grill, and eat at home. At seven o'clock, I will go to the movies in town.

Or set in commas and add a coordinating conjunction.
   I eat, sleep, do homework in the morning, and go to school.

I could add a semicolon.
   I eat, sleep, do homework; then I go to school.

L. Learn to correct illogical coordination.

For example:
> Swimming in the lake, because the water is warm, and my sunburn hurts, may give me relief.

I have incorrectly coordinated a clause "because the water is warm," a phrase "swimming in the lake," and a word "relief." I need to coordinate all of these, so they become the same. I can rearrange the phrases "swimming in the lake," "with warm water," "may give me relief from my sunburn."

1. I could use all clauses.

   Because I am swimming in the lake and because I have a sunburn, I may get some relief.

2. I could use all words.

   My swim in the lake with my sunburn may give me relief.

Exercise 121

A. Create your own sentence with illogical coordination as in my example in the previous page. Then rewrite it correctly in one of three ways: with phrases, clauses, and words.

B. Now create another sentence with illogical coordination, then rewrite it correctly in three ways: with phrases, clauses, and words.

M. Dangling Modifiers

When you use words to modify other words, keep them close together; otherwise, the meaning may be lost. The modifiers dangle like grapes on the vine when they are not put clearly together with the words they modify.

For example:
Children should be aware of car traffic when they are driving. (This sounds like the children are driving the car.)

It would be more logical to write this:
Even though they are driving in the car, children should be aware of traffic.

We have moved the modifier "when they are driving" closer to the children. The modifier no longer dangles.

Rule 69

The rule is to keep the modifying words or phrases close to the word that you are modifying.

Here is a sentence that is unclear. You could interpret it many different ways.
The difficult book's language was very old.

Is this sentence about the book that is difficult to read, or is it about a book with an old language? If I position the modifier closer to the book, it will become clear.
The book's difficult language was very old.

Knowing what you like, quickly I order breakfast.
What happens quickly, what I know, or what I order? I place the modifier *quickly* closer to the verb, *order*.
Knowing what you like, I quickly order breakfast.

Only is an adverb that is often left dangling.

What do I really mean with this sentence? Does it mean not to work if you do not receive money, or does it mean that I should only work if I need money?

I need to place *only* directly before the word or phrase it modifies.
Work only when you receive money.

After doing her homework, Janet and I went for a walk.
Does this mean that Janet and I did her homework, or that we went for a walk together after she did her homework?

An unmistakable meaning would be this:
After Janet did her homework, we went for a walk.

Exercise 122

Change the following dangling modifiers to make unmistakable sentences.

1. Snowboarders should be aware of skiers when they cruise down the mountain.
_____

2. The long walk´s path was very windy.
_____

3. After listening to her complaint, Jean and I went to the store.
_____

4. Taxi drivers should be aware of trucks when they change lanes.
_____

5. The complicated discussion's conclusion was indisputable.
_____

English Workbook for Grades Six to Eight

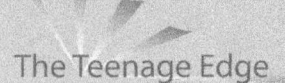

Irregular Verb List

Present Tense	Past Tense	Perfect Tense
arise	arose	arisen
(be) am, is	was, were	been
beat	beat	beaten
become	became	become
begin	began	begun
behold	beheld	beheld
bend	bent	bent
bereave	bereaved, bereft	bereaved, bereft
bid	bade, bid	bidden, bid
bind	bound	bound
bite	bit	bitten
bleed	bled	bled
blow	blew	blown
break	broke	broken
breed	bred	bred
bring	brought	brought
build	built	built
burn	burnt, burned	burned, burnt
burst	burst	burst
buy	bought	bought
cast	cast	cast
catch	caught	caught
choose	chose	chosen

Present Tense	Past Tense	Perfect Tense
cling	clung	clung
come	came	come
cost	cost	cost
creep	crept	crept
cut	cut	cut
dig	dug	dug
dive	dived or dove	dived
do	did	done
draw	drew	drawn
dream	dreamed, dreamt	dreamed, dreamt
drink	drank	drunk
drive	drove	driven
dwell	dwelt, dwelled	dwelt, dwelled
eat	ate	eaten
fall	fell	fallen
feed	fed	fed
feel	felt	felt
fight	fought	fought
find	found	found
flee	fled	fled
fling	flung	flung
fly	flew	flown
forbid	forbade	forbidden
forget	forgot	forgotten
forgive	forgave	forgiven
forsake	forsook	forsaken
freeze	froze	frozen
get	got	gotten, got
give	gave	given

Present Tense	Past Tense	Perfect Tense
go	went	gone
grind	ground	ground
grow	grew	grown
hang	hung, hanged	hung, hanged
have, has	had	had
hear	heard	heard
hide	hid	hidden
hit	hit	hit
hold	held	held
hurt	hurt	hurt
keep	kept	kept
kneel	knelt	knelt
know	knew	known
knit	knitted, knit	knitted, knit
lay (to place)	laid	laid
lead	led	led
leap	leapt	leapt
learn	learned	learned
leave (to depart)	left	left
lend	lent	lent
let	let	let
lie (to recline)	lay	lain
light	lit, lighted	lit, lighted
lose	lost	lost
make	made	made
mean	meant	meant
meet	met	met
mistake	mistook	mistaken
overcome	overcame	overcome

Present Tense	Past Tense	Perfect Tense
partake	partook	partaken
pay	paid	paid
put	put	put
raise (elevate)	raised	raised
read	read	read
rend	rent	rent
rid	rid	rid
ride	rode	ridden
ring	rang	rung
run	ran	run
say	said	said
saw	sawed	sawn
see	saw	seen
send	sent	sent
set	set	set
sew	sewed	sewn
shake	shook	shaken
shave	shaved	shaved, shaven
shear	sheared	sheared, shorn
shed	shed	shed
shine	shone, shined	shone, shined
shoe	shod	shod
shoot	shot	shot
show	showed	shown
shrink	shrank	shrunk, shrunken
shut	shut	shut
sing	sang	sung
sink	sank	sunk
sit	sat	sat

Present Tense	Past Tense	Perfect Tense
slide	slid	slid
sling	slung	slung
slink	slunk	slunk
slit	slit	slit
sell	sold	sold
seek	sought	sought
sleep	slept	slept
smell	smelt, smelled	smelt, smelled
smite	smote	smitten
sow	sowed	sown
speed	sped, speeded	sped, speeded
spend	spent	spent
spill	spilled, spilt	spilled, spilt
spin	spun	spun
spit	spat	spat
split	split	split
spoil	spoiled, spoilt	spoiled, spoilt
spread	spread	spread
spring	sprang	sprung
stand	stood	stood
stick	stuck	stuck
stink	stank	stunk
strew	strewed	strewn
stride	strode	stridden
strike	struck	struck, stricken
strive	strove	striven
sweep	swept	swept
swell	swelled	swollen, swelled
swim	swam	swum

Present Tense	Past Tense	Perfect Tense
take	took	taken
teach	taught	taught
tell	told	told
think	thought	thought
thrust	thrust	thrust
thrive	throve, thrived	thriven, thrived
tread	trod	trodden, trod
understand	understood	understood
weep	wept	wept
wind	wound	wound
withhold	withheld	withheld
withstand	withstood	withstood
write	wrote	written

Figure 16.

Preparing for Tests

When you are faced with a test, pick a partner or a group to help you learn the contents on the test. You probably need someone to help you figure out what you know and what you do not know. To do this, let someone ask you questions and test you. Then you need to practice what you are unsure of.

For example, if in two weeks' time you have a test on the grammar of pronouns, conjunctions, and clauses, find yourself a partner or a group of partners, and ask each other what you know and what you do not know. Read the book if necessary. Figure out how the language works.

Make a quiz or a practice test for the others, and ask them to make one for you. Once your partner has taken your test, correct it for her.

The next time you meet, figure out what you know and what you are still unsure of. Then make an agreement with yourself on how you are going to learn that grammar. The agreement should be honest, realistic, and may be difficult. If you like, show the agreement to your partners, and see if they agree. The final step is to help each other succeed in fulfilling the agreements.

Once you have taken the test, you will learn the most important thing – the types of mistakes you tend to make in English. Make sure you learn from all of your mistakes. If it is a spelling mistake, write each word three times. Should it be a punctuation mistake, learn the rules! If it is a grammar mistake, write the sentence correctly.

Sample English Test

I. The Verb Matrix
1. Write one sentence in the past continuous tense.
2. Write one sentence in the past perfect tense.
3. Write one sentence in the future continuous tense.

II. Special finite verbs
4. Write a negative sentence with *may.*
5. Write an interrogative sentences with *can.*

III. Mood
6. Write one sentence in the imperative mood.

IV. Infinitives
7. Write two sentences with the infinitive *to.*

V. Participles
8. Write one sentence using a continuous participle as an adjective.
9. Write one sentence using a perfect participle as an adjective.
10. Write one sentence using a continuous participle as an adverb clause equivalent.

VI. Adjectives
Adjectives used attributively add something to the noun. Write sentences using the following adjectives attributively.
11. new
12. lovely

Write sentences using these adjectives as nouns.
13. brave
14. blind

Write sentences using adjectives with the following suffixes.
15. -ous
16. -less

VII. Adverbs
Write sentences with adverbs that:
17. Describe the verb.
18. Describe the adjective.
19. Describe the adverb.

VIII. Pronouns
Write sentences with the following pronouns.
20. one

21. so
22. such
23. less
24. both

Write sentences with the following relative pronouns.
25. who
26. whom
27. whose
28. which
29. that

IX. Conjunctions
Write sentences with the following coordinate conjunctions:
30. so
31. but
32. yet
33. for
34. nor

Write sentences with subordinate conjunctions.
35. after
36. before
37. when
38. as

Write sentences with the following correlative conjunctions:
39. either or
40. neither nor
41. but also
42. no sooner than

Index

Adjectives 14
    Coordinate 120
    Cumulative 120
    Demonstrative 89
    Forming the negative 71
    Interrogative 74
    Order of 120
    Position of, 12
    Possessive 73,86
    Used as nouns 67
    Used attributively 12,65
    Used predicatively 66

Adverbs 14,76
    Adverbial phrases 83
    Comparison of 79
    Game 83
    Of affirmation 76
    Of frequency 12,82
    Interrogative 76
    Modify adjectives 80
    Modify verbs 8
    Of manner 12,82
    Of negation 76
    Of place 12,82
    Of probability 76
    Of quality 76
    Of time 12,82
    Position of 12
    With prefexes 78
    With suffixes 78

Adverbial phrases 13,18

Antecedent 104-106
    As a word 104
    As a phrase 104
    As a clause 104

Appositives 31

Articles 14

Charles Dickens
    Oliver Twist 44-45
    Great Expectations 124

Clauses
    Adjective clauses 21,29,30,39,43
    Adverb clauses 21,34,42
    Analysis of 42
    Conditional clauses 23,37,43
    Dependent clauses 9,10,11,21,22,42
    Independent clauses 9,10,11,19
    Main clauses 9, 21
    Non-defining, adjective clauses 39
    Noun clauses 21,31,32,42
    Relative clauses 26,30
    Restrictive and non-restrictive clauses 38-42

Complement 11,31,53

Complex sentences 9, 22

Compound sentences 8,9

Conjunctions 8,14
    Coordinating 8,9,116
    Correlative 118
    Subordinating 9,117

Constitution of the United States 124-126

Direct and indirect speech 119

English
    American 7,39,119,122
    British 7,39

Fragmentations 127-145
    Dangling modifiers 143
    Illogical coordination 143
    Mixed constructions 140
    Sentences 142

Improper Shifts 127
    In mood 130
    In number 127
    In person 127
    In pronouns 128
    In speech 136
    In tenses 129
    In tone 138

In voice 135

Indirect object 60

Indirect speech 136-137

Interjections 14

Mood 49
    Conditional 49
    Imperative 49,132
    Improper shifts 132-134
    Indicative 49,132
    Interrogative 49
    Subjunctive 49,130

Nouns 14
    Appositives 63
    Grammatical function of 60
    Gerund 60
    Position of 11
    Possessive form 62,
    Used as adjectives 68

Object 17
    Direct 11,17, 60
    Indirect 11,60
     Of the preposition 11,60
     Of the verb 31,53,60

Paragraph 10,123

Parallel structure 139

Participles 55-59
    As adjective clause equivalent 58
    As adverb clause equivalent 58
    Compound 56
    Past with regular verbs 55
    Perfect made with irregular verbs 146-151
    Perfect active 55
    Perfect passive 56,57
    Position of 58
    Present passive 56
    Progressive 55
    Used as adjectives 57,70
    With infinitive 57

Parts of speech 14

Phrases 18-19
    Adjective phrases 18
    Adverbial phrases 18,83
    Gerund phrases 61
    Noun phrases 18
    Parallel structure 139
    Prepositional phrases 18, 141
    Verb phrases 18

Predicate 17

Predicate adjectives 31

Prefixes 71

Prepositions 14, 107
    And adverbs 113
    Game 108-109
    Group 108
    Of place 108
    Of time 111

Pronouns 14
    Both 93
    Demonstrative 89
    Distributive 97
    Improper shifts 128
    Indefinite 91
    Intensive 84
    Interrogative 100
    Other, another 94
    Possessive 86
    Reflexive 84
    Relative 9, 20, 26-29,
    So, one 87-88

Punctuation
    Colon 119
    Comma, uses of, 8,9,73,121,123
    Dash 121,122
    Ellipses 122
    Exclamation marks 121,123
    Hyphen 121
    Parentheses 122
    Question mark 121,123
    Quotation marks 121, 122,123
    Semi-colon 119
    Slash 122

Sentences,
- Affirmative 93
- Analysis of 17
- Complex 9
- Compound 9
- Compound-complex 10
- Interrogative 94
- Negative 94
- Simple 9
- Structure 8

Subject 11, 17

Subject – predicate combination 18,19

Suffixes 68

Tense of Verbs
- Future simple 6
- Future Progressive 6
- Future Perfect 6
- Future Perfect Progressive 6
- Past Progressive 6
- Past Perfect 6
- Past Perfect Progressive 6
- Past Simple 6
- Present Progressive 6
- Present Perfect 6
- Present Perfect Progessive 6
- Present Simple 6
- Shits 129

Tests 152-154

Verbs 14
- Irregular verb list 146-151
- Infinitive 52, 53
- Regular 55
- Phrasal 115
- Shall 7
- Special finite 48,52
- Transitive and intransitive 46
- Voice 135
- Will 7
- With prepositions 47

Word position 8

Congratulations, now you have completed this workbook!

Please contact me at:

Ted Warren

www.teenage-edge.org

email: ted.warren@teenage-edge.org